Hot cottage collectibles

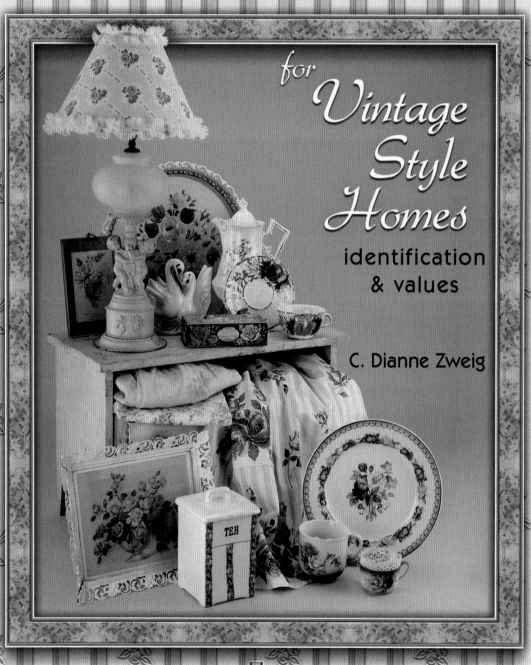

for *Vintage Style Homes*

identification & values

C. Dianne Zweig

COLLECTOR BOOKS
A Division of Schroeder Publishing Co., Inc.

Cover design: Beth Summers

Book design: Lisa Henderson

Cover photography: Charles R. Lynch

The examples of cottage style collectibles featured on the cover are part of the author's collection and can be found at the Collinsville Antique Company, www.collinsvilleantiques.com, a 22,000 square foot antique emporium in New Hartford, Connecticut. For inquiries visit www.cdiannezweig.com or email the author at Dianne@cdiannezweig.com.

* The author's website cdiannezweig.com was designed by bzine studios, www.benzweig.com.

COLLECTOR BOOKS

P.O. Box 3009
Paducah, Kentucky 42002-3009

www.collectorbooks.com

Copyright © 2009 C. Dianne Zweig

The current values in this book should be used only as a guide. They are not intended to set prices, which vary from one section of the country to another. Auction prices as well as dealer prices vary greatly and are affected by condition as well as demand. Neither the author nor the publisher assumes responsibility for any losses that might be incurred as a result of consulting this guide.

Searching for a Publisher?

We are always looking for people knowledgeable within their fields. If you feel that there is a real need for a book on your collectible subject and have a large comprehensive collection, contact Collector Books.

Proudly printed and bound in the United States of America

Contents

Dedication

In Loving Memory

Beatrice Segal

1930 – 2007

About the Author

Dianne who lives in a home decorated in "cottage style of unknown origin" is working very hard to "re-purpose" (cottage jargon for recycle) all the junk her kids brought home from college. When she is not cleaning out cluttered rooms and closets she can be found at her computer working on books and articles about "hot" collectibles and other subjects that capture her attention. Her first book, *Hot Kitchen & Home Collectibles of the 30s, 40s, 50s* (collectorbooks.com) was very well received and convinced her that she was up for another challenge. Dianne, an author, mixed-media artist, and psychotherapist has been collecting and selling cottage collectibles in Connecticut for over 27 years. Her number one pastime

The author (1950s) in the arms of her mom, Beatrice Segal.

is travelling around her home state and beyond, visiting her favorite antique shops, galleries, and eateries. Dianne's articles on collectibles, the psychology of collecting, and home trends appear regularly in many local, regional, and online sites. To read Dianne's latest articles or to learn more about where you can find Dianne's collectibles to purchase, please visit her website at www.cdiannezweig.com if you would like to contact dianne, email her at Dianne@cdiannezweig.com.

In Recognition

The author wishes to recognize the wonderful contributions of Charlie Gifford (photographer) and Ella Williams, two very special people. Charlie and Ella worked with Dianne on her first book and continued to help Dianne with this project until their unexpected passing (2007). They will be missed dearly.

Special thanks to the gals at the Plantsville General Store Antique Center, Elaine, Pam, Ann, Cathy, and the rest of the sisterhood, thanks for your friendship and support.

Acknowledgments

First I would like to thank my computer for hanging in there with me during all kinds of ups and downs. During the last week of preparing this manuscript I nearly flipped when the keyboard was typing strange combinations of words. Convinced I had just entered the twilight zone and would be unable to complete this project I screamed in an absolute panic to my in-house "techy" son Ben..."HELP." He screamed back "batteries"... "put new batteries in your keyboard!" Whoa... I didn't even know it used batteries. I was so happy this dilemma had a happy ending.

Why didn't my new smart computer tell me in advance what was going on? The printer talks to me all day long, letting me know what color ink I'm getting low on. On the subject of ink...I used up plenty of it printing out contact sheets of the photos contributed by over 50 collectors and dealers of cottage collectibles. (See Contributor & Resource List in the back of the book.) This book happened because all of you made it happen. I facilitated the project, but you all made this happen with your enthusiasm, professionalism, and expertise! Besides chatting with these gals online and by phone all the time

Courtesy of www.preservecottage.com.

about cottage collectibles, I also had the opportunity to get to know some of these women more personally and I am truly enjoying our friendships.

The following people kept me sane (in order of appearance into my life): Pam Kaplan of preservecottage. com; Pam Daly of vintagepastelle. com; Karen Corazzelli of cottagerags. com; Deb Schrodt of pinkpigwestport. com, Maureen and Reuben Reid of arosewithoutathorn.com. These contributors were there from the beginning and went way out on a limb for me over and over again... and goodness knows there were times I was hanging from a limb! Thanks to you all... you were all a gift from Heaven. Artists Ronda Juniper Ray, Alice Wingerden, and Jo-Anne Coletti were gracious with their time offering design consultation and contributing photographs.

I wish to acknowledge the excellent staff at Collector Books. They are an author's dream team. It's a pleasure to work with Gail Ashburn, editor; Amy Sullivan, assistant editor; Beth Summers, art director; and Lisa Henderson, designer.

Thanks to my daughter Leah, and son Ben, and to my husband Richard for helping with research, proofreading, and technical support.

How This Book Is Organized

Following some helpful introductory chapters on what cottage style is and how to accomplish this look with the collectibles, furnishing, and accessories you buy and use, I present the main portion of this book, hot cottage collectibles and furniture.

These trendy collectibles will be covered in 12 distinct chapters representing a variety of themed cottage styles as well as typical collectibles associated with cottage style in general.

When relevant, I have shared with the reader interesting facts and commentary on cottage collectibles and cottage style

living. I have flagged for the reader those items that are extremely popular and have included additional resources for readers who want to go further in their research on a particular topic.

Of course it is important to point out that this book contains photographs from collectors all over the country and a few even from Australia (I have adjusted their values to American dollars). Each photograph is captioned with the contributor's website address.

This book contains a pretty good cross section of the country so that you will be able to see for yourself that there are indeed ranges in what things cost in different areas. To find a particular photo contributor, refer to the list of Contributors & Resources in the back of the book. If you need further help with an item shown, you may certainly contact these wonderful cottage collectors directly. I found all of them to be conscientious, gracious, and informed collectors and sellers of cottage collectibles.

I should also mention that if a collectible was inadvertently listed with a price that is too low or too high, or you find some other error, please accept my apology. This was of course unintentional. Please use this book as a guide, not a bible.

Courtesy of www.preservecottage.com.

In closing, I do want to point out the challenge of developing a book which covers so many different kinds of antiques and collectibles. To really get the concept of "cottage," you need to see the total picture not just the individual items alone. So I have included photographs which have illustrated how "cottage" looks when you put it all together. This is not typical for a price guide, but this was the best way for me to help readers not only learn something about the values and identification of objects but also offer some ideas about how to use and display these very same collectibles.

Acquiring a Taste for Cottage

For those of you who had an opportunity to read my first book, *Hot Kitchen & Home Collectibles of the 30s, 40s, and 50s,* you know that my love of kitchen collectibles had a lot to do with the cherished times I spent in Grandma Sophie's red and yellow kitchen. Grandma Sophie was my mom's mom. In my second book, *Hot Cottage Collectibles for*

Vintage Style Homes, it is dad's mom, Grandma Esther who seems to have influenced my long-held interest in cottage kitsch and relentless collecting. Her presence in my early life also seems to explain further why I prefer paper over china and flea markets over fancy auction houses. I'll get to that piece shortly.

But first I want to tell you how I learned about cottage décor. Way before Rachell Ashwell, who founded Shabby Chic in 1989 and introduced the world to flea market décor, there was "Shabby Grammy," my grandmother Esther who introduced me to "Bingo Chic."

Her expertise in cottage style living was a direct result of her uncanny ability to win at Bingo. Follow along with me.

Each summer, Grandma would join our family on our annual summer vacation in the Catskill Mountains of New

York, aka "The Borscht Belt." Every afternoon at 2:45 P.M. Grandma would grab her change purse and head for the bingo hall for the 3:00 game. After the game, she often returned to our cramped bungalow with her arms filled with "collectibles of the future" (Bingo prizes).

Her yield might include a ceramic cheese tray with a matching set of spreaders, salt and pepper shakers, coffee mugs, candy dishes, etc. If this wasn't enough of a thrill for anyone, she would also attend the evening games and return with even "better and bigger prizes."

Grandma Esther was a very colorful person, literally! She would wear a red sweater, purple chunky beads, green earrings, and a multicolored crocheted hat with a matching scarf, and somehow made it all work together. For a person whose clothes often came from a rummage sale, she looked marvelous! If you wanted to learn how to mix and match anything, all you had to do was study Grandma. She gave me my first lessons on mixing textures, fabrics, patterns, colors, and styles, a key element of cottage style decorating.

My grandmother also taught me a great deal about "junking," a term many collectors use to describe their compulsion to shop at tag sales, salvage yards, and second hand shops. She didn't need to step out of her door to shop; "the junk" came to her. People gladly brought their "heirlooms" to grandma. She was the quintessential scavenger, who collected everyone's hand-me-downs from glassware to dishes and from old linens to moth eaten blankets. Boy how I wish I held onto her pocketbook collection.

So you see, my dad's mom was way ahead of everyone in her understanding of cottage style living. With a great deal of ingenuity, Grandma could take everyday objects, what collectors and designers call "flea market finds" and create the Taj Mahal. She also had a knack for bringing life back to discarded furniture, linens, and textiles. She really was the first in the family to appreciate the value of distressed coffee tables, chippy painted night stands, faded drapes, lamps with replaced shades, and rusted wrought iron plant stands.

I spent a lot of time with my Grandmother Esther, the matriarch of odds and ends, so it makes sense that she would have a big influence on my tastes for collectibles and décor. By the way, while I am on the topic of taste, I must confess that

besides my early experiences with "Bingo Chic," there are other reasons why it hasn't been easy for me to develop a taste for "expensive taste."

I prefer paper and plastics over glass and ceramics. My propensity for using cheap disposables is a habit I developed from my dad who learned it from "Shabby Grammy." Dad, mom, and grandma used white paper plates with ruffled edges to serve the hot dogs they sold in their luncheonette. After all how would a frankfurter with mustard and sauerkraut served with a side of French fries and a big sour pickle look on fine china with hand-painted roses? Growing up I didn't get a lot of exposure to porcelain and crystal. I do however know a lot about how many sizes paper coffee cups come in and which plastic lids work the best.

While I have always been "china challenged," I have experienced a breakthrough as a result of writing this book and talking to seasoned romantic cottage collectors. My husband thinks my recent shopping sprees are purely for "research purposes only" and will cease once my book is in print. Obviously he is not as well acquainted with the psyche of a collector as I am. My buying frenzy will taper off when three things happen:

- I run out of shelf space to display my collections
- There is no more Tupperware to giveaway to free up more closet space for my new acquisitions
- The compulsion to use paper and plastics overtakes me.

Cottage Roots

While everyone has a different take on cottage homes, most people think of cottages as cozy dwellings near the beach, out in the country, or tucked away in the mountains. For my family our cottage was a humble vacation bungalow in either Loch Sheldrake or Monticello, New York, during the 1950s. These towns are located in New York's Catskill Mountains. Home to numerous bungalow colonies, the mountains were where

families from the city migrated each summer. Bungalow colonies in the Catskill's were a haven for Jewish families who had experienced exclusion and discrimination in other places.

Older guests would hire a hack (private car) to take them to the country. Hacks would leave the city packed with people, leaving no room for baggage which was generally sent up separately by truck or with younger family members who arrived earlier.

Heading to the country, wherever that might be, was a tradition for many families. Mothers would hope that by leaving the city, their children would breath in fresh air and be less likely to contract polio, tuberculosis, and other serious diseases. Early cabins had front porches which were generally open and enclosed in later years when the threat of disease lessened (Mulfinger and Davis, 2003).

Many bungalow guests started out first in what was referred to in Yiddish as a "Kochalain," a summer boarding house with cooking privileges. To be able to afford to stay in your own bungalow meant that you were doing well. Even so, bungalows were cramped as several generations might share the same one or two room cabin with the younger ones sleeping on cots or day beds in the kitchen.

Despite cramped cabins, the country was also the place where you woke up to the sounds of birds chirping, the smell of fresh morning air, and the chatter of your friends and cousins who lived in the bungalow next door. Their bungalow was directly across from their grandmother's bungalow who shared a backyard with your neighbors from back home.

In the Catskills, bungalows or cottages were organized in colonies or campgrounds for groups of families and friends who all knew each other and over the course of several generations vacationed together.

While all these cabins were quite small and compact, they all had their own identity. Owners equipped and decorated their cabins with hand-me-down curtains, gently soiled tablecloths saved for the country, and furniture left behind from someone else's cabin or a bought at a yard sale.

As you might imagine, some bungalow owners with a knack for "bungalow chic," like my very own "Shabby Grammy," were able to transform their temporary summer quarters into lively, adorable, and charming vacation homes while others preferred their cabins plain and simple. Everyone however came to the country to relax and forget about spills, dust, clutter, and chores. Laundry hung on a line outside a short distance from the rusty swing set, weathered see saw, and crowded sand box where children played while mom or dad organized a card game, shuffleboard match, or volleyball tournament.

When supper was finished and young children were in bed, parents would sit on the porch and enjoy a cup of tea and small talk with friends and family. If someone happened to "smuggle" in a newspaper into the campground, this was also a time to catch up on what was happening back in the city. But for the most part, bungalow colonies offered a break from television, radio, and the outside world. Summers were for flowers, fresh air, and communal living.

Bungalow Living in the Country

As you have already heard, Grandma Esther was a very resourceful person when it came to homemaking and personal style. "Shabby Grammy" knew how to improvise and stretch a dollar in every facet of her life, work, home, apparel, cooking, etc. In the bungalow kitchen, Grandma could create three course meals from what most of us throw out. Grandma Esther was the perfect person to take with you to the country where survivor skills are essential.

O.K., I'm exaggerating here. You didn't really need survivor skills in the country, but you did need a well rounded indoor-outdoor type who could swat mosquitoes, concoct family meals in a kitchen the size of a shoe box, and handle plumbing emergencies without a meltdown. Grandma Esther was such a person. She came equipped with a variety of fly swatters, an assortment of mix-matched dishes and pots, and her trusted personal toilet plunger. All of these gems had been accumulated over many years and brought to the country during the summer months

packed away in boxes labeled "summer."

Just like her ability to put herself together with colorful clothes from a rummage sale, Grandma Esther could also keep everything together in our bungalow and back home for that matter. When she returned to the city she worked in a bakery well into her eighties. An active octogenarian she also boarded a bus by herself and travelled for hours to visit grandchildren, always toting a pink bakery box loaded with cookies. In the country grandma rocked lots of baby carriages and kept an eye on her family. Grandma enjoyed country living and helped all of us experience a pleasant summer in our home away from home.

Overtime, bungalow colonies aged as well as the folks who set up camp summer after summer. Grandma Esther lived well into her nineties and left behind lots of stemware, scarves, and souvenirs. All the kids who played together outside our bungalow in the Catskills grew up, went off to college, married, and established families of their own. Sadly these young families would not have an opportunity to return to their summer cottages as many colonies began to disappear, being sold off at foreclosure rates. While a few hotels remained in the area, many former bungalow guests headed away to other vacation spots.

Grown-up Cottage

After a short stay in Florida, I exchanged palm trees for evergreens and moved up north to New England. We missed

the Catskills but found a new mountain getaway in southern Vermont. For many years our family rented a mountain hideaway, slope side, where our kids could ski on and off right outside our door. It was easy for the kids to return to the cabin for a hot chocolate or a change of clothes. In the evening we would prepare a simple dinner of pasta and salad and play board games or assemble jigsaw puzzles on the coffee table in front of the fireplace. These memories of all of us together in the living room of this vacation house are very precious.

Re-creating Warm & Cozy

By the time I completed this book, I was more convinced than ever that cottage style was not a catchy phrase coined by savvy designers but really a state of mind that is catching on in many circles. When you are in the cottage zone, old is new again, comfortable trumps formality, and romantic adds a lovely touch. Finally you can take the plastic coverings off the sofa and curl up with a good book. Or, you can put your feet up on the coffee table without concern. Perhaps you want to set your glass down without a coaster, go ahead… it's cottage time, 24-7! Close your eyes, you are back in your favorite old bungalow or vacation cottage where fresh air and laid back living is what the doctor ordered. Well maybe not your doctor, but it's high on my list of suggestions. Cottage style collectibles and furnishing are hotter than ever because it seems that everyone is ready for time off. This book has been developed for the growing number of people just like you (and me) who yearn to escape from their hectic worlds and who are more than ready to kick back, unwind, and relax surrounded by the people, pets, and collections that make them happy… enjoy… it's cottage time!

Cozy Is Back in Style

Cottage style living is having a comeback. At the time of this writing an article in the *Boston Globe's* Real Estate section titled "A Cottage Comeback" discussed the rise in home developers who are creating 1,000 square foot homes for both young professionals and empty nesters in "colony" settings across the country. Touted as affordable and cozier alternatives to condos and large homes, cottages are back in style. Like the cottages of yesterday, today's new cottages are built without attics, basements, or a full second floor reminiscent of the classic Cape Cod cottages built for whalers and fisherman by ship carpenters.

There has been a rise everywhere in the establishment of adult self-contained lifestyle communities catering to folks who want to escape city life and return to quieter vacation type settings. Small is the new big. Now there seems to be a complete turn around in what many home buyers are after (or can afford).

Smaller, easy to maintain cottage type homes with built-ins, nooks, and charming décor in clustered neighborhoods are all the rage for older couples, singles, and small families, while "McMansions," a term used in the *Globe* article mentioned earlier, is for the growing family.

Courtesy of www.preservecottage.com.

It seems that everyone wants a cottage of their own. For $199.00, you can buy your kids a child's size plastic "Country Cottage" by Little Tikes Company (ages 2 and up). This charming house with a full-size door has been updated with modern conveniences such as a pretend swivel faucet, stovetop with clicking knobs, and a push-button play phone. I am surprised this successful toy company hadn't added a pretend flat screen television so little ones could feel at home. Or is that the point… leave out the high tech distractions such as televisions, cell phones, and computers… for a more cottage-y experience?

I grew up before the days of Little Tike. If I wanted to play house, my sister and I had our favorite sheets and blankets which we draped over tall pieces of furniture to create our tent house. The biggest thrill was when dad made us baloney sandwiches with potato chips and we ate them inside the tent.

Children, like pets, enjoy finding dark cozy places to hide away in. How envious I am of Opie, my geriatric Sheltie, who can be found tucked away in the closet behind the laundry basket, curled up quietly in his favorite corner. I imagine he has found a way to escape my teenager's loud hip hop music or he is still aggravated because I moved his water bowl to make room for my new refrigerator. By the way this stainless steel refrigerator is so big and industrial looking that my older son refers to it as "a space ship." This modern appliance from another galaxy would be a tight squeeze in a cozy cottage. One would have to consider a smaller model for a 1,000 square foot home.

But trust me, there are plenty of people willing to give up a few cubic inches in their refrigerator size for a chance to find peace and quiet in a mountain retreat, beach cottage, or lake cabin.

Small is the new big. Bookstores are now stocking many more titles on hideaways, tree-houses, cabins, cottages, log cabins, bungalows, houseboats, small spaces, etc. These are not books for children; these are books for adults that can be found in the interior design, architecture, and home remodeling sections of major book chains. You can also buy plans to build your own treehouse or order the parts for your very own cottage. There are schools turning up to teach people how to build and equip a log cabin. I actually found a website that featured pre-fabricated cottages that you could order online. I'm giving this serious thought… I want an art studio!

Why are small, cozy cottages back in vogue? Is the interest in living simple and small directly related to how complicated and large our lives have become? Some psychologists say that our interest in living in cozy cottages has deeper meaning than simply wanting an affordable alternative to large homes.

What psychologists have found is that our early experiences with building or creating "first play homes" (tents, huts, hideaways, secret havens) stays with us as pleasant reminders of places that were safe, comfortable, and private.

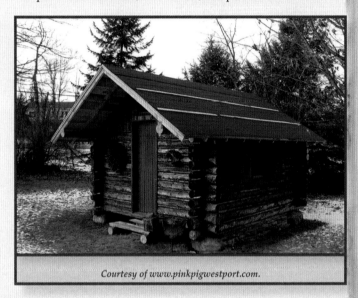

Courtesy of www.pinkpigwestport.com.

We develop bonds not only with these pretend houses but also with the full-size spaces we grew up in. According to Clare Cooper Marcus, the author of *House: As Mirror of Self*, "a home fulfills many needs: a place of self-expression, a vessel of memories, a refuge from the outside world, a cocoon where we can feel nurtured and let down our guard."

Perhaps this is why cottage style living is becoming so attractive… it is allowing people to play once again and create personal spaces that are fun, cozy, and manageable.

What Are Cottage Collectibles?

So what are cottage collectibles? From my vantage point, as a compulsive shopper of cottage chic (flea market finds), "cottage" is all your mother's or grandmother's stuff re-packaged and mixed with your great-grandmother's heirlooms and creatively blended together with the "stuff" your kid's brought home from college or you found on your own. In other words, "cottage" is a look which marries different periods and styles together, so that a pretty Victorian era tea set can be used on a forties hand-embroidered tablecloth atop a one-of-a-kind country style table in a seashore cottage. Cottage taste is eclectic and varies from frilly to rustic and everything in between. What makes up this "look"… everything!

Forget about your vision of Hansel and Gretel's whimsical cottage in the woods with charming windows and sweet hand-painted kitchen chairs and tables. That look was retired with your Slinky and Tinker Toys. Today's cottage collector is way beyond the fairy tale stage.

Cottage collectors are realists. They know that sooner or later one has to find a clever way to explain what they call all the odds and ends they have accumulated and arranged for years in their cluttered homes. Influenced by more famous pack racks and trendsetters, cottage caught on as a genuine style which emphasizes comfort, practicality, whimsy, and creativity.

Let me clarify further what is meant by the phrase "style." When antiques, collectibles, textiles, wall covering, etc. are grouped together by similar appearance, material, structure, time period, function, etc. they form a "style." Cottage style can be applied to several different unique themes including romantic cottage, country cottage, rustic cottage-cabin, beach-seaside cottage, retro-whimsical cottage, etc. While each of these versions of cottage have their own dominant features and elements, they all emphasize a relaxed, inventive, and timeless approach to décor and lifestyle. I will also add, that cottage style is very popular today because it is affordable.

While one can certainly try to replicate a bungalow from the Arts & Crafts era and get into some hefty dollars buying art pottery, designer furniture, and architectural elements consistent with that style, this book is a more general guide for obsessed collectors like you and me. This is not a book about buying Rookwood vases or Stickley furniture. This is a book about using your Aunt Sylvia's old silverplated teapot as a vase and giving new life to your mom's end tables.

More and more I am coming across buyers who are passing up brand new manufactured furniture for older pieces which they transform to meet their needs. Even vintage furniture dealers are catching on. Why sit with an old table from the 1950s or earlier when you can sand it, paint it white, add some charming knobs, and offer it as a rea-

Courtesy of The Bleu Willow.

sonable alternative to the higher priced, imported, inferior products being mass produced today?

The beauty of cottage collecting is that the sky is the limit... you can collect all of it, use it instead of just look at it... and make it all work together. Your kitchen can resemble a French country cottage while your den can look like it came out of a cabin in the Adirondacks. Or your house can look like mine... cottage of unknown origin! That is what happens when your college kids graduate and use your house for storage.

Cottage style is not just for baby boomers with downsizing in-laws. Even younger generations are re-creating their own sense of cozy by recycling, transforming, and embellishing hand me downs and discards. Cottage style is elevating "junk" to "junque" and delighting collectors everywhere by allowing them the freedom to experiment, expand, and re-interpret home décor and objects of desire.

Bedroom-side table.
Courtesy of www.preservecottage.com.

Courtesy of Ronda Juniper Ray.

Many people credit Shabby Chic creator Rachel Ashwell for introducing the world to cottage style where faded, time-worn textiles and affordable collectibles are mixed with elegant and stylish décor. Her brand founded in 1989 became a retail success story as well as a decorating style which continues to influence industries, collectors, and designers worldwide.

Following Rachel Ashwell's lead you will find an entire cottage industry of vintage cottage collectors who buy and sell floral textiles, patchwork pillows, hand embroidered linens,

Courtesy of www.lavenderhillstudio.com.

crystal chandeliers, chippy furniture, ornate accessories, hand-painted china, and other romantic cottage favorites. Many of these businesses have formed networks online which cater to vintage and romantic chic buyers.

While Rachel Ashwell has warmed the hearts of so many of you who are reading this book, I want to emphasize to my readers that other interior designers have also had an impact on what is hot and what is not. Ralph Lauren popularized the handsome British country look with jewel-tone colors, textured fabrics, and leather furnishings.

Pierre Deux, which started out as a quaint Provence-themed antique shop in New City in 1967, has become a prominent company known for their country French textiles and furnishing associated with the French countryside. Small print fabrics, distressed furniture, and comfy upholstered pieces with palettes of sunny yellow, bright blue, and deep reds are just some of the elements of this cottage style.

Martha Stewart and Mary Engelbreit are household names. Women all over America and beyond, pay close attention to what Martha and Mary have cooked up for us to try in our own homes. Both have greatly influenced our ideas about cottage style living. In fact if Martha features a new use for a particular collectible, she can shake up the antique world for weeks, driving prices sky high for what was previously a forgotten treasure. Ask any dealer who has lived through one of these frenzies.

Women everywhere are building forts out of piles of back issues of Martha's *Living* magazine and Mary's *Home Companion* which they hold onto... "for the ideas." I'm still thinking about giving a new life to old metal office furniture with a fabulous green re-do, just like Martha did in one of her feature articles. If only I had more time to "shabby-tize" the ugly office desks sitting in my basement. First I would have to find the desks which are buried under all the "hot collectibles" I couldn't resist.

So let me return to the question I started with. What are cottage collectibles? Cottage is whatever you want it to be. When you are thinking "cottage," you are having fun! There are no rules... so kick back, snuggle up, and enjoy reading about cottage collecting. You will find over 900 photographs inside this book from over 45 of the top cottage collectors around. Take it easy today... tomorrow is a very busy day... tomorrow you will be out hunting for more stuff!

Types of Cottage Styles

Step one in the process of becoming a true cottage style collector is to decide what type of cottage style appeals to you. This will make the hunt so much easier. Let's face it, you cannot unleash an obsessed collector into the world without some specific instructions or they will return home with everything but the kitchen sink and maybe even the sink as well, whether they need it or not!

The charm of cottage collecting is that if you like variety, this is a perfect way to keep you busy hunting. Trust me, you will never get bored. You can collect miniature lighthouses for your "beachy" bathroom, scout about for a chippy frame to make into a mirror for your bedroom, or search for a colorful camp blanket for your rustic den. There is no limit to how much fun you can have accessorizing your home or building nifty cottage style collections.

What follows is a simple listing of the variety of cottage styles which are popular today with a brief summary of what collectibles are generally associated with each style. Throughout this book I will discuss in much more detail the elements and collectibles that characterize each distinctive style.

Beach cottage: Plenty of pastels, whites and creams, nautical accessories, weathered flea market finds, shabby furniture, seascapes, tropical influences.

Rustic: Back to nature, dark stained furniture, reclaimed woods, cabin influences, wool textiles.

Country: Baskets, enamelware, open shelves and cupboards, quilts, painted or pine furniture, floral arrangements, folk art, small print fabrics, ruffles, lots of exposed collections. Country can also be further narrowed to English, French, Southwest, etc.

Whimsical: One-of-a-kind colorfully painted furniture, decorative kitsch, objets d'art, funky collections, patterns, bright palettes. Mary Engelbreit touches.

Retro: Often found in beach cottages because the 1950s were known for plastics and pastels. Mid-century influences, collections of quirky ceramics, barkcloth textiles, paint by number paintings, etc.

Shabby chic: A mixture of floral fabrics, slip cover white or pink furnishings, pretty layered bedding, crystal chandeliers, chippy or rusted accessories, flea market finds. Think Rachel Ashwell here.

Victorian country also known as romantic country: The feminine lighter side of Victorian mixed with classic country. Lots of florals, layered textiles, elegant touches, decorative plates, hand-painted china, ornate, detailed accessories.

Cottage Style Basics

When considering the principles of design whether referring to a painting or looking at a room's interior you will often hear the term "design elements." These are the basic components of design which make up the whole picture. They include color, texture, pattern, scale, light, and shape or form. Cottage style decorating favors certain elements that characterize this look. As discussed earlier there are many types or sub-categories of cottage style such as country, rustic, retro, etc. to name a few.

Even with a wide range of overall style options, there are still many easily identifiable features which have come to be associated with cottage style collectibles and décor. This section is devoted to helping you think more about these popular cottage basics.

Words that you will often see used to describe a cottage feeling: worn, torn, shabby, comfy, tattered, used, sweet, charming, casual, light, airy, vintage, fresh, rusty, chippy, relaxed, informal, handmade, nostalgic, soft, cluttered, busy, fresh, and at times whimsical and colorful. You will learn more about particular elements listed below in upcoming chapters where you will find plenty of examples of furniture, collectibles, and textiles which are so cottage-y!

Furnishings

Here are very common elements associated with cottage style furnishings:

- Painted furniture (full range of possibilities see color)
- Chippy, flaky, peeling painted surfaces
- Second hand furniture and flea market finds
- White or pink painted furniture for romantic looks
- Armoires and interesting cabinets, dressers, and desks
- Incorporating lots of antiques and collectibles
- Slipcovers
- Overstuffed comfy chairs and sofas
- Ottomans
- Distressed furniture
- Surfaces show weathering
- Mixing different periods and styles of furniture
- Chips, scratches, dings, imperfections are welcomed
- Cottage furniture such as farm tables, cupboards, cabinets
- Repurposed furniture, i.e. using a Hoosier cabinet for a computer station

- Painted cabinets, charming knobs, open look to see collections
- Vintage blanket chests, trunks, boxes
- Campy, Adirondack furniture for rustic looks
- Wrought iron
- Headboards from salaged items such as picket fences, grates, etc.
- Lots of wicker, garden ornaments, porch accessories

Colors

While you can really choose a palette which works for you, here are some favorite cottage color options.

- Lots of greens (celadon, gray-green, seafoam)
- Pastels and soft tones
- Crisp white, creamy whites
- Neutrals, sandy beige, khaki, straw, wheat, putty
- Romantic pinks, salmon, buttery cream, robin blue
- Classic blue and white
- French palettes of sunny yellow, red, blue
- Colorful exciting colors for whimsical and retro cottages
- Patriotic colors of red, white, and blue

Interior designer Betsy Speert's book *Great Color & Pattern Collection*, Meredith Books, is a great resource for the Cottage style collector who wants to learn more about using color and pattern to organize collections.

Betsy's chapters on colors showcase rooms that are done in red, blue, green, yellow, brown, neutral, white, and black. Within these categories she shows the reader what colors complement the main color chosen and what collectibles and objects are also compatible. She does the same in her chapters on pattern, dividing these areas into toiles, floral, plaids and checks, stripes, and found pattern.

Pattern & Textiles

Here are the many different ways to create a cottage-y feeling using textiles. Use:

- Lots of florals
- Chintz
- Calico
- Toiles
- Plaids
- Stripes
- Gingham
- Chenille

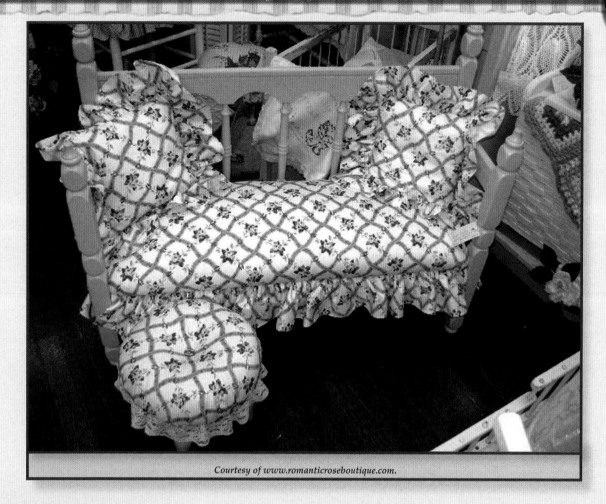

Courtesy of www.romanticroseboutique.com.

- Mixing different patterns together
- Ruffles, trim, and handmade accessories
- Lots of cushions and pillows
- Making pillows from old tablecloths, bedspreads, etc.
- Using quilts and blankets as tablecloths
- Using vintage embellishments
- Layering fabrics and textiles
- Patterned wallpaper
- Throws, quilts, coverlets
- Skirting vanity areas, etc.
- Hand-embroidered linens
- Making window treatments from vintage fabric, old tablecloths, etc.
- Valences and cornices to add charm
- Using baskets, burlap, rattan, and wicker for texture

Form (walls, ceiling floors, architectural trim)

- Reclaimed wood surfaces (and furniture)
- Salvaged architectural trim, old shutters, doors, windows, etc.
- Exposed beams

- Using old doors as room dividers or backdrops for accessories
- Beadboard
- Using old windows to paint on
- Stenciled walls
- Open shelving with collections
- Mosaic or tile backsplashes
- Painted walls, floors, and accessories (sponging, crackling, pickling, staining, washing, faux finishes)
- Wood floors with area rugs
- Floor cloths
- Handmade rugs
- Natural fiber rugs

Lighting

- Vintage lamps with shabby shades
- Crystal chandeliers
- Italian tole
- Sconces
- Funky lighting
- Lamps made from unusual finds.
- Soft lighting for romantic cottage looks

Courtesy of www.shabbyvilla.com.

Famous Cottage Communities

Catskill Mountains

Earlier, in the section called Cottage Roots, I discussed the popularity of the bungalow colonies of the Catskill Mountain region of New York State. A tradition for families for many generations, beginning in the early part of the twentieth century, these once-thriving campgrounds are almost all gone. Starting out as chicken and dairy farms, these settlements grew from boarding houses to bungalow colonies welcoming guests summer after summer (Brown, Phil, 2002). For additional information on the Catskills visit http://catskills.brown.edu/.

Wesleyan Grove in Martha's Vineyard

Campground living is common for many other groups as well. Visitors to Martha's Vineyard get off the ferry in Oak

Bluffs and within a few minutes walk are delighted to see approximately 315 cottages remaining in Wesleyan Grove, a Methodist camp-meetings grounds. There, religious revivals lasting several days necessitated temporary housing for worshippers. Originally tents erected in circles were evolved into wood-sided, wood-framed canvas topped structures which later developed further into cottages. If you visit the site today you will be charmed by colorful Carpentar Gothic style cottages with lots of gingerbread trim and front porches with painted rockers. These cottages are owned privately now and are no longer quarters for worshippers.

A visit to Wesleyan Grove feels like you have just been transformed into Mary Engelbreit's storybook world where cottages painted pink and yellow or purple and green or red,

white, and blue dazzle your senses and awaken your fondest a childhood memories. The desire to get a peak inside one of these cozy, quaint dwellings is overpowering. In my last visit to the island I had to settle for a long chat with a gentleman relaxing on his open porch.

Cape Cod

Many of the early cottages were originally built for whalers and fisherman by ship carpenters. These small dwellings were named for the region and were called Cape Cod cottages. Simply constructed along the New England coast in the eighteenth century, Cape Cod cottages were influenced by English architecture. Built as single story or story and a half small homes, these classic capes were designed to be moved by horses if land and sea conditions changed. Unlike the Carpenter Gothic cottages discussed earlier, these cottages lacked ornamentation and had interiors resembling a ship's cabin with a center fireplace to warm the home and allow for cooking. Weathered shingles and a gable roof were typical.

New and re-furbished cottages are built with classic and traditional designs maintaining the original look of these seaside communities (Plante, Ellen, 2000).

Nantucket

Cottages with white picket fences and window boxes with colorful flowers are similar to the ones found on Cape Cod but also show influences from the Quaker settlers. Box shaped homes with gray shingled exteriors are common. Thousands step off the ferry which brings visitors to the island and walk on cobble stone streets to shop in quaint boutiques surrounded by boatyards and residential communities.

Cape May, New Jersey

Just like the cottages in Oak Bluffs at Wesleyan Grove, visitors to Cape May will find cottages with Victorian architecture. Built at the height of the Victorian era in the 1800s, these cottages are adorned with carved barge boards, ornate trim, and fancy porches which invite guests and a warm community feeling.

Where to Find Hidden Cottage Treasures

With so many people collecting is there anything left to find and where are some places to check out? I have to chuckle when I think about this topic because I came across this little paperback a very long time ago that dealt with this subject and had some rather bold ideas to suggest for collectors. One of these ideas was to study people's porches and notice which ones had lots of clutter on them. The author recommended ringing the door bell and asking the home owner if they were ready to part with their old rocker or chest or barrel. I actually still focus on porches but I haven't knocked on any doors yet.

Besides the obvious places to visit such as shops, auctions, tag sales, flea markets, and eBay, there are other stops to consider for bargains. Try salvage yards, consignment shops, thrift stores, pawn shops, swap meets, dumps, rummage sales, and bankruptcy sales.

The key to visiting many of these haunts is going often and going early in the day or week. Ask folks at these places if they have a schedule for when they put out new items. One local shop I visit is closed on Mondays and Tuesdays and generally has new finds unpacked on Wednesdays. You want to try to learn how each shop operates. Many people have figured out a good way to be the early bird buyers at local thrift shops. These clever folks offer to volunteer and help sort out and price items that are donated. Some dealers even offer their appraisal services for free in exchange for a preview of new goods. Most charity shops welcome more help so go ahead and sign up.

Another way to discover hidden treasures is to look in your own basement, garage, or attic. I have met many people who have made cleaning out these storage areas a thriving business, picking out some of the favored pieces for themselves and selling off the rest at flea markets on the weekends. Offering to help run an annual tag, book, or rummage sale at a local church, synagogue, or community center or even helping out a neighbor's sale is another way to find collectibles early in the game. If you need some extra money you might want to work part-time in a multi-dealer shop or for an auction house. These are two great ways to keep abreast of fresh inventory and learn more about your area of interest.

Ron, an expert scavenger and a dear friend of mine, has had great success finding "jewels" going underground if you will. He is not afraid to go digging in discontinued landfills, old battlefields, and historic sites (not government regulated). He also combs town records for sites which once had very old homes, hotels, or buildings built on them and are now empty lots. After mapping out his adventure he recruits his sons and they are off for another one of Dad's archeological digs.

Networking is an important way to learn about similar collectors of the particular item you may be looking for. A really effective way to find desired items is to simply place an ad in your local paper or leave your business card in local shops.

Lately a lot of people are having tremendous success using craigslist a community based online classified network started in 1995 by Craig Newmark. Originally started as a hobby, craigslist is now used by 30 million people monthly in 450 cities worldwide. According to craigslist's information fact sheet, if you can believe this, there are only 25 employees working out of a Victorian house in the Inner Sunset neighborhood of San Francisco. While it is free to use craigslist, they support their operations by charging below market fee job ads in 10 cities and brokered apartment listings in New York City www.answers.com/topic/craigslist.

Craigslist has a very active list of people buying and selling collectibles, furnishing, and even store fixtures such as glass display cases. Recently, I decided to try posting a listing on craigslist. It was so simple. It worked like a charm. Let's face it, people read this online network. Do I have to tell you the obvious… keep your pilot light on when wheeling and dealing online. Of course this applies to all types of transactions, doesn't it?

Courtesy of The Bleu Willow.

Building a Collection "a la Cottage"

Many people love to build collections and even have multiple collections. Cottage style is perfect for the eclectic collector. Often collections start forming quite accidently. But before long, a decision is made to actually build your room(s) around this collection. Or the opposite occurs, you decide on a particular type of cottage style and then you slowly add collectibles and decorative accessories to form the look you are developing. If you intend to follow a specific style, I might suggest building your collection(s) with some planning. For some people approaching "the hunt" with some structure helps them organize their field trips. If you are new at this, perhaps it might be helpful to review the section on Types of Cottage Styles and to think about what fits your personal taste.

Next, I would suggest becoming familiar with the collectibles and furniture featured in this book as well as other books and magazines on the subject. Then you will have an easier time spotting a real good find and having some sense of what the values are. I have included in the back of this book a very helpful comprehensive bibliography which is divided into specific categories about cottages and collectibles. You will find many excellent resource books on this list which I found extremely helpful.

When you are out scouting for collectibles to add to your cottage collections or room décor, take a few pieces from your exiting collection with you. I can often be found walking around an antique mall or group shop with an arm full of objects to see how individual items look together. These are the times I find out quite accidently that a color or pattern I never dreamed of using with what I have, looked quite well when all my odds and ends were laid out on the table.

Or, sometimes all you need is to add a tiny touch of a stronger color to an object you have found. For example, suppose you find a patterned lamp shade which is so close to what you want but a little too soft in color. Don't give up... add a delicate ribbon in the color you need around the top or bottom edge of the shade to accent the shade and give it some punch. In cottage style you make it work... one step at a time. That is the thrill of cottage style you can keep building and rebuilding your collections!

Courtesy of www.pinkpigwestport.com.

Courtesy of the Bleu Willow.

How to Display, Store & Use Vintage Finds

All About Walls
Using Wallpaper in Cottage Style Homes
Lining Drawers, Shelves, Room Dividers with Wallpaper & Fabric
Textures, Textiles & Images Added to Walls
Changing Wall Surface
The Wall as a Support (surface for hanging)
Three-Dimensional Collections Displayed on Walls
Creating Support (walls & backing) from Other Materials
What's "Hot" in Salvage

Hooks, Tacks & Coat Racks Made from Vintage Finds
Coat Racks & Hall Trees
Hooks & Curtain Tie Backs

Cabinets, Cupboards & Fitted Displays
Cabinets with Cubbies, Drawers & Partitions

Shelves & Horizontal Displays

Storage
In the Kitchen, Pantry & Utility Room
In the Den, Living Room & Study
In the Bedroom, Vanity & Sewing Room

Courtesy of www.shabbyvilla.com.

Making the Transition to Cottage Style

Are you a Sunday collector, or is your mission to convert one or more rooms of your house into a particular cottage style? Most people who get hooked on the cottage thing are doing both, they are slowly upgrading or is it downgrading some of their rooms and also accessorizing them with collectibles and furnishings. I am using the term "downgrading" humorously to illustrate how cottage style allows folks to replace their formal furnishings with more casual, comfy alternatives.

If your ultimate goal is to live more comfortably you may want to begin by taking inventory on what you want to keep, what you want to ditch, and what you can make-over in the spirit of living the cottage life. Room by room, one baby step at a time, it is helpful to make a list of what is hot and what is not. This is actually the fun part. You look at what you have and imagine it differently. Are your bedroom lamps really tacky or do they have potential if only you added some cute shades? Should you buy a new bookcase or "shabby-tize" the one you have with a different color and finish?

Once you get into the cottage mode, the sky is the limit. Now you can look at grandma's coffee table with a whole new vision. Suddenly 1940s dated can become retro-romantic chic with the right touches or you can transform old architectural salvage into some eye-catching decorative accessories.

To help you make the transition into cottage style, I would like to share with you some terrific ideas about how to change what you have, how to display and store your collectibles and décor, and how to be on the lookout for vintage finds which are so cottage-y. I thank Pam Daly of vintagepastelle.com and Marilyn Krehbiel of hannahstreasures.com for their input in preparing this section. You will also find numerous examples of vintage wallpaper in many upcoming chapters as well as other ideas to help you on your way to cottage style collecting.

I do want to mention that just days before I was ready to submit this book project to my publisher, a pleasant surprise arrived in the mail. The lovely staff at Old House Interiors sent me a copy of *Old-House Interiors Design Center Sourcebook*. This is the companion book to oldhouseinteriors.com. For anyone interested in vintage home interiors and exteriors their annual reference guide is an excellent source for finding both antique and reproduction hardware, salvage, wood, flooring, textiles, ceilings, trim, furnishings, fixtures, appliances, etc.

All About Walls

Using Wallpaper in Cottage Style Homes

Walls can become an interesting display all by themselves even without objects. Vintage wallpaper, texture, fabric, tiles, murals, faux painting, collage, etc. can all be used to create exciting accents to a plain and empty wall.

One of the best ways to replicate a particular type of cottage style is to bring original colors, patterns, and textures into the room. You can buy vintage wallpaper or reproductions of older patterns being made for today's consumer.

Here is what you can do with wallpaper or vintage fabric.

- Frame fireplaces and window walls with wallpaper.
- Use novelty papers (lighthouses, sailboats, sea shells) in bathrooms in beach cottages.
- Frame smaller pieces of nursery themed wallpaper. Most repeats are 18" and 19" tall, within that repeat there could be several images that could be individually framed to make a grouping.
- Paper half of a wall and incorporate wainscoting or a chair rail.
- Use wallpaper in the kitchen as a backsplash accent between the counter tops and cabinets.
- Use a matte sealer to the wallpaper after hanging to protect the surface from spills and slashes.
- Select vibrant botanicals from the 1950s look great in retro cottage homes or mixed with wicker.
- Cover room screens with florals, botanicals, and other vintage wallpaper patterns.
- Line the drawers of vanities, desks, old dressers, etc. with small patterned papers in soft colors… very romantic cottage.

Lining Drawers, Shelves & Room Dividers with Wallpaper & Fabric

Wallpaper (and fabric) is not just for walls. Wallpaper is ideal to line your drawers, cabinets, shelves, room screens, armoires, etc.

Spruce up some old drawer interiors with some pretty

Shabby cabinet from vintage window and distressed wood, $45.00. Courtesy of www. LisasCraftiqueBoutique.com.

on, or change their surface with painting techniques, plaster, mediums, and other products which are easy to work with. You can apply texture, color, and even embed objects (flowers, leaves, memorabilia) into these products by using special tools and materials. For helpful advice on how to go about changing wall surfaces, visit your local paint store or large fine art outlet.

In kitchens and around fireplaces, tiles are very lovely additions for a cottage look.

Vintage wooden drawer from old sewing machine painted white, distressed, decorated with roses, and lined with floral fabric, $39.00 – 45.00. Courtesy of www.soshabbypink.com.

Room screen with vintage botanical wall-paper, $145.00. Courtesy of The Bleu Willow.

vintage wallpaper to create a particular style of cottage. For example, for a tropical look, perhaps a 1950s botanical is what you are after for your cottage room screen. Or maybe a small print pink floral design is just the touch needed for your soft romantic bedroom or vanity dresser drawer.

Textures, Textiles & Images Added to Walls

Textiles such as fabric, burlap, blankets, and area rugs make great wall coverings too. Vintage fabric fastened to one or more walls in a room is a lovely way to bring in color and texture. You can cover an entire wall or use a vintage shawl, article of clothing, tapestry, or carpet as a center of interest.

Images from old books, magazines, catalogs, newspapers, etc. can be collaged on walls. Victorian era postcards and calling cards are delightful examples of vintage paper also known as ephemera which can be used.

Changing Wall Surface

Early country cottages were built with inside walls made of stone, rough plaster, wood, packed earth, etc. Exposed beams and palettes of terra cotta, ochre, or neutrals were common for interiors. Today you can mimic the older looks with a little creativity… (o.k. maybe a lot of creativity).

Walls are like blank canvases which you can stencil, print

If you want to have some fun, try your hand at "pique assiette," broken china mosaics. Shards of broken plates look great on a kitchen backsplash. (See the chapter of Romantic Dining-One of a Kind for more about this art form.)

Vintage kitchen cupboard door, embellished with vintage china plates, $125.00 – 150.00. Courtesy of www.lavenderhillstudio.com.

hand-held vanity mirrors, Hawaiian shirts, paint by number paintings, hats, quirky plates with different edges and shapes, vintage tin children's beach shovels, mirrors with a variety of frames and shapes, old skeleton keys, souvenirs, tole trays, orphaned pot covers, and vintage garden tools.

The Wall as a Support (surface for hanging)

Walls can also be used as surfaces or supports to hold collections. Hanging pictures and collectibles is tricky, but once you let yourself experiment you can have a ball creating exciting displays. Unless an object is large or a painting is prominent, one small picture hung by itself looks lonely.

Pairs and groupings work better. Recently I hung four identically framed black and white pen and inks in a row on one of my kitchen walls. Mounting them in a line gave the room a more contemporary look. You can also stack pictures two on top and two on the bottom or other combinations of numbers. When objects share something in common they form a pleasing ensemble. One collector showed me how she grouped dozens of vintage wedding pictures of different couples together. Because all of the photographs had a theme to them, they formed an interesting collection.

A large collection of small flea market paintings all with different frames can also work well if the overall look is a wall filled with similar sized frames. In this formation you are spacing pictures equally apart but arranging them together as you would a jigsaw puzzle. This type of mounting works well on the walls bordering staircases.

Three-Dimensional Collections Displayed on Walls

Pictures, prints, and paintings are not the only way to decorate a wall. Three-dimensional objects can also be used quite effectively. You can hang objects in a straight row, vertically, or randomly using hooks, pegs, brackets, and small ledges. The more unexpected the objects are, the more exciting the presentation can be. This is where kitsch and unusual objects have a place in organized displays. Here are just a few ideas to consider as wall décor: antique beaded pocketbooks, jewelry, small

Creating Support (walls & backing) from Other Salvage Materials

Cottage style decorating is all about coming up with creative ways to recycle a variety of interesting materials. Many salvage pieces can be turned into charming walls, backboards, mirrors, and supports for artwork or they can be used to hang collections or household items. Throughout this book you will see the work of artists Jo-Anne Coletti and Ronda Juniper Ray as well as others who have mastered the art of painting on old weathered, chippy windows, door panels, cabinet doors, etc. You can also use salvage items as room dividers which can add character to a cottage style home. Of particular interest to collectors these days are architectural salvage which has layers of paint a chippy finish. For those of you who are new to the word "chippy," I am referring to painted surfaces which are weathered or peeling.

The flaking paint is very cottage-y.

Chippy painted old shutter, single, $12.00. Courtesy of The Bleu Willow.

Old door panel, chip paint, $40.00. *Courtesy of The Bleu Willow.*

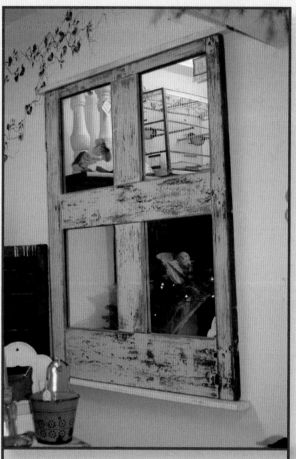

Old window, painted, converted to mirror, $145.00. *Courtesy of The Bleu Willow.*

Old shabby window hand painted with pink roses by artist Jo-Anne Coletti. Can be used as wall dedor or even a room divider. Window, $25.00; w/artwork, $175.00. *Courtesy of www.vintagerosecollection.com.*

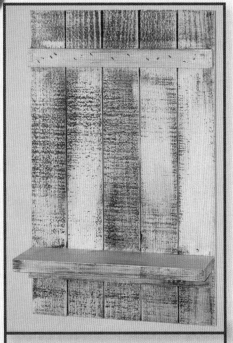

Barn door, chippy white paint, $150.00 – 200.00. Courtesy of Country Cottage Florist.

Shelf made from old cabinet door, $20.00. Courtesy of www.lisascraftiqueboutique.com.

Door panel, vintage painted with garden theme, $125.00 – 150.00. Courtesy of Country Cottage Florist.

Thumb latch doors, 1" thick, $125.00 each. Courtesy of www.Vermontsalvage.com.

Old shutter hung from ceiling makes a great surface to hang collections from and also serves as a room divider, $40.00. Courtesy of The Bleu Willow.

What's "Hot" in Salvage?

So what exactly should you be on the look out for at salvage yards, flea markets, junk shops, antique shops, etc.? Today's shopper is after many different kinds of salvage and vintage items which can be used in a variety of ways. Here is what is "hot" right now: old shutters, lattice, gates, grates, garden trellis, retired baby crib rails, picket fences, cabinet doors, full size doors, old windows, pegboards, chicken wire, screen doors, and windows, and fabric room screens. Cottage collectors may decide to keep these items in their original form with peeling paint, rusted and rough surfaces, and even broken parts or to re-paint, restore, and change their appearance. Once you find some neat salvage such as a rusty gate or a splintering shutter, then what? You can use these items to hang collections on or in the lingo of cottage style, "re-purpose" them into new uses. Of course these unique supports also work quite well for organizing garden tools, utensils, pictures, keepsakes, gadgets, and kitchenware. Antique corbels, porch post and columns, architectural salvage also can also be used as pedestals or shelf, table, and room divider components. Many people like to use an interesting grate or gate simply as wall décor or a bed headboard.

In bathrooms, try transforming an old window into a mirror over the sink. You can then use the frame around the mirror to display memorabilia or a pin back button collection. Pam Day of vintagepastelle.com is enamored with old picket fences which she uses to make whimsical garden or porch benches. I have included one of her benches in this section, but you will find others in the chapter called Country Garden. While I'm talking about gardens, you can also take something that was intended for outside and bring it inside. A nice old weathered garden trellis can have many uses indoors especially as a lovely backdrop for holiday or floral decorations.

Red painted shutters, can be used as decorative accessory or cute backdrop, $25.00. Courtesy of Country Cottage Florist.

Old garden trellis (common type) creates some interest over the office area of this shop. Can be used for hanging objects, holiday decorations, or dried flowers, $25.00. Courtesy of The Bleu Willow.

Old garden trellis, hand-made, with charming design qualities, $125.00. *Courtesy of The Bleu Willow.*

Old shutters with chippy paint, $45.00 each. *Courtesy of The Bleu Willow.*

Large picket fence bench, 1930s, wood, original hand-painted creation, $195.00. *Courtesy of www.vintagepastelle.com.*

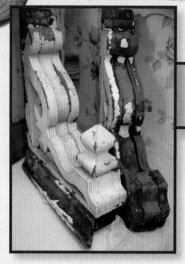

Antique corbels from Victorian home, 16" x 13" at the base, $65.00 each. *Courtesy of www.teacupsandtwigs.com.*

Hooks, Tacks & Coat Racks Made from Vintage Finds

Turned porch posts and columns, Victorian, $85.00 each. *Courtesy of www.vermontsalvage.com.*

- Tole candleholders can be used as hooks for lingerie or dried flowers.
- Drill a hole in an old spoon, fork, or knife, and then bend into a charming wall "hook."
- Glass door knobs mounted on a wall make nifty holders for so many objects.
- Sconces are decorative ways to hang things.
- Hatpins are attractive to use for tacking papers, vintage postcards, photographs.
- Decorative vintage hardware can be mounted on a wall to hang things from.
- Look for vintage curtain tie backs, they make charming "thumb tacks."
- Attach vintage hooks to old tin ceiling tile.
- Make a neat coat rack from a vintage door.

Coat Racks & Hall Trees

Coat rack made from vintage salvaged door, hardware, and hooks, $75.00. *Courtesy of www.teacups and twigs.com.*

Coat rack made from a salvaged door with old door knobs, $95.00. *Courtesy of www. teacupsandtwigs.com.*

Antique, weathered three-pane window converted to hanger with decorative painting, antique decorative back-plates and new porcelain knobs, window unpainted, $20.00 – 30.00; after converting to coat rack, $200.00. *Courtesy of www.bellarosadesigns.com.*

Vintage hall tree made from old door with antique mirror, silver tray inset, old legs, $395.00. *Courtesy of www.teacupsandtwigs.com.*

Hooks & Curtain Tie Backs

Italian tole strawberry hook, 1950s, original paint, strawberries, $30.00. Courtesy of www.vintagepastelle.com.

Wall hooks, mounted on antique ceiling tiles and painted, $30.00 – 35.00 each.
Courtesy of www.pinkpigwestport.com.

Tulip tie back, 1930s, celluloid tulip push pin for curtains, $10.00 pair.
Courtesy of www.vintagepastelle.com.

Cabinets, Cupboards & Fitted Displays

Painted farm style or cottage cabinets are very desirable at this time. I have noticed an increase in the popularity of painted wood cabinets refinished with pastel colors. An old pie cabinet that has been refinished in a sage green and cream wash is hot, the same cabinet in a dark primitive look is not.

Corner cupboards can be given an updated look by painting two different colors on the inside and outside. Today

I visited a shop where a typical corner cabinet that you might find in grandma's house was transformed into an exciting decorative piece. Painted with flat black paint on the outside and flat white paint on the inside, the piece took on a contemporary look. The owner then accessorized this piece with funky red, yellow, and white collectibles transforming this once drab cabinet into a nifty piece for a whimsical cottage look!

Next to this cupboard stood an old farm cabinet painted a very striking color of jade. When I opened up the doors to this cabinet I was pleasantly surprised to find them painted red and the cabinets shelves left unpainted. It was a neat looking vintage find with a modern flair. The owner sat a charming child's rocker painted red on top of the cabinet and I fell in love with the color combination of red collectibles and a jade cabinet.

You see you need not think of cottage as simply soft pastels. Cottage style is all about mixing it up so that you playfully combine colors, time periods, and collectibles. Perhaps this cabinet was once used in a country kitchen. Now it might find a new home in a den, playroom, or bedroom.

Art Deco cabinets are also having a comeback. They look especially funky in retro-styled cottage kitchens. Colorful Fiesta ware and vibrant 1940s and 1950s tablecloths make a great combination. Vintage wardrobe cabinets are great for storing linens.

Cabinets with Cubbies, Drawers & Partitions

People love salvage and older items which can be made into shelves and cubbies. Older boxes that have partitions are especially sought after because they can be mounted on the wall and converted into a great "cabinet" for display. This past week I sold a lovely older box which was used to ship champagne bottles in. The buyer fell in love with the engraved

writing on the outside of the box sides and the shelves that formed when the box was stood upright. Old tool totes make wonderful shelves when they are also turned on their side.

Be on the lookout for cabinets and furnishings with lots of drawers or cubbies which may have been used in an entirely different way than today's cottage collector might envision. There are so many uses for old spice cabinets, vintage mail sorters, pharmacy cabinets with lots of drawers, hardware cabinets, old library card catalog cabinets. Linda Campbell and Ann Vaughn, owners of The Cottage Well Loved are very successful with selling old step back cupboards, post office cubbies, and cabinets of all kinds which they repurpose, lingo among cottage collectors for finding new uses for old items.

Instead of changing the use for a cabinet you can also completely change its appearance. Vintage medicine cabinets can be repainted and collaged to charm cottage powder rooms and vanity areas. Never toss old magazines and newspapers or other vintage paper, they can be used in so many fresh ways. See photo shown in this section.

Hard to find cabinet from a New York hardware store, excellent condition, $3,000.00 – 5,000.00. Courtesy of www.arosewithoutathorn.com.

An old cubby from a hardware store atop a baker's cupboard base. The cubby, $98.00; the cupboard base, $365.00. Courtesy of www.cottageatleesburg.com.

Medicine cabinet, 1930s, wood, shabby style, collaged, hand painted, vintage perfume labels, $145.00 – 165.00. Courtesy of www.vintagepastelle.com.

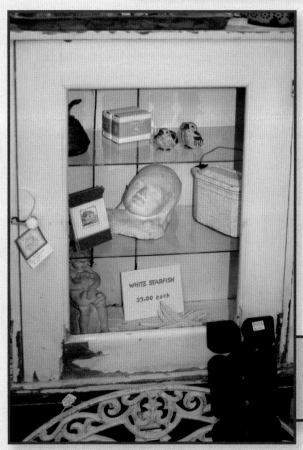

WHITE STARFISH
$3.00 each

Primitive cabinet, glass shelves added, front door panel removed, $125.00 – 135.00. Courtesy of The Bleu Willow.

Shelves & Horizontal Displays

Many flat surfaces are available for displaying collectibles and décor. Shelves, windowsills, mantles, the top of beams, on top of kitchen cabinets, tables, and chests, etc. They can be used to group collections. Collections can be arranged with objects of similar color, shape, material, era, or use.

When displaying mixed objects in a collection or objects of different size, also experiment with using different levels. For example, create height by placing an object on top of a few vintage books or old tin. Another way to build interest is to have some objects come forward on a shelf and some recede behind. To accomplish this you may want to create a background object. Here is a suggestion to get you thinking about styling your collectibles. Perhaps you might take a pretty vintage hand-painted plate and set it upright on a small easel. Then you can choose a complementary object to set in front of it. This brings out the color and creates a backdrop. In my

shop, I will often set a colorful cover from a magazine, vintage toy box, game board, book, or piece of vintage fabric to make an interesting display.

It's always fun to change your displays. Some people enjoy using the seasons as a time to re-arrange their collections. Pastel colored florist vases from the colorful era look so pretty grouped together and are a lovely change after the winter holiday months. White pottery of different sizes and shapes form an elegant collection in any room and any time. Candlesticks mixed and matched are also a classic way to go. These collectibles are easy to find and still reasonably priced.

Shelves can be the collection themselves. Pam Day of vintagepastelle.com likes to think "in and out of the box!" Her shelf shown in this section is really a collection made from several different vintage items fastened together. Her unique "shelf" is made from an old frame with glass added, salvaged wood, and accessorized with vintage doll furniture.

There are so many ways to create shelves. Here are some ideas:
- Bookcases can be turned upside down and mounted on the wall.

- Old stepladders make adorable stands for planters and other small collectibles. Shutters can be made into very durable shelves.
- Boxes can be mounted on the wall and used as shelving.
- Painted vintage children's chairs can be mounted on the wall and used as a shelf to hold a favorite doll, a plant, stuffed animal, etc.
- Hang an old children's swing from the ceiling and use as a shelf.

- Mount a vintage doll-size dresser on the wall and use as a shelf.
- Insert glass shelves into a vintage birdcage and use as a quirky "showcase."
- An old cornice can be converted into a shelf or flower box.
- Attach a small shelf to the side of an armoire to store small items or for display.

Cute handmade red painted stool is a great shelf, $24.00. Courtesy of The Bleu Willow.

Red and yellow step ladder, 1940s, $28.00. Courtesy of The Bleu Willow.

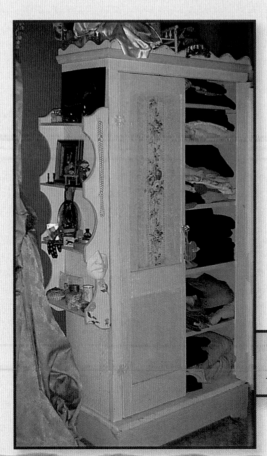

Small shelf attached to the side of an armoire to store small items or for display, $25.00 – 45.00. Courtesy of www.vintagepaselle.com.

Old stepladders make adorable stands for planters and other small collectibles. *Courtesy of www.preservecottage.com.*

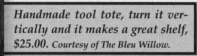

Handmade tool tote, turn it vertically and it makes a great shelf, $25.00. *Courtesy of The Bleu Willow.*

Shelves can be made from several different vintage items fastened together. The unique collage shelf is made from an old frame with glass added, salvaged wood, and accessorized with vintage 1920s doll furniture, 1905 catalog cover etc., $85.00. *Courtesy of www.vintagepastelle.com.*

Storage

Cottage style is a planned mishmash with lots of collections, mixed and matched accessories, textiles, and furnishings. Clutter is something entirely different.

When you walk into a room and see piles of old newspapers everywhere, on chairs, countertops, tables… that is clutter. Take these same newspapers and store them in a charming hand-painted box which you "shabby-tized" and that is cottage!

Hand-painted vintage wood box, $65.00 – 75.00. Courtesy of www.natashaburns.com.

In the Kitchen, Pantry & Utility Room

One of the worst places for clutter is drawers, especially kitchen drawers.

Here is a typical scenario. You can't pull out your kitchen drawer because it is jammed with so many "freebies" that you picked up at last year's town fair. You know what I am talking about… the rubber jar openers that have the wrong political party on them, the measuring spoons with the local realtor's name imprinted on the handles, the wooden spoons that you burnt and forgot to throw away. You try to pull out a ladle and you have to go through an obstacle course. That is clutter.

Now what are some other ways to help you think like a cottage style collector so that you can organize all these odds and ends?

- Use colorful 1940s floral vases to hold kitchen utensils.
- Hang pots and pans from the ceiling.
- Hang kitchen utensils on the wall.
- Vintage candy, apothecary, pickle, and Hoosier jars make good canisters.
- Use lid-less teapots to hold pens and pencils.

- A vintage mail sorter or old wooden pie box can store papers, mail, etc.
- Utilize the top of kitchen cabinets for collections, serving trays, platters, baskets, batter bowls, etc.
- Display everyday dishes in an old open European plate rack mounted to the wall.
- Chimney cabinets with charming painted doors are great for storing tools.

In the Den, Living Room & Study

- Store newspapers and magazines in old boxes and baskets.
- Old trunks, chests, or suitcases can be used as tables and also provide extra storage.
- Create window seats with drawer storage in window alcoves and accessorize with colorful barkcloth cushions and pillows.
- Orphaned vintage hutches can be painted or refinished and placed on top of a desk or table to store books, hold collections, or be used as an organizer.
- Old Hoosier cabinets with enamel tops are great computer stations.
- Vintage butlers' cabinets without the shelves can conceal a television.
- Vintage tin or tole garbage cans can store rolls of wallpaper, remnants of material, etc.
- Vintage planters and waste baskets store magazines and fabric.

This vintage tole garbage stores wallpaper and fabric remnants, $30.00 – 60.00. Courtesy of www.vintagepastelle.com.

Christie Repasy, rose basket, 1950s, wood decal signed, $65.00. Green Majolica planter, 1915, as found, $50.00. Courtesy of www.vintagepastelle.com.

In the Bedroom, Vanity & Sewing Room

- Pretty vintage floral hatboxes are great for storage.
- Use items in new ways, a vintage tea canister can hold cotton, a planter can hold razors.
- Hang necklaces on lampshades and watch the light shine through glass beads.
- Drape jewelry on mirrors.
- Vintage butlers' cabinets without the shelves can conceal a television.
- Fasten jewelry, and drape necklaces and scarves on vintage dress forms.
- Store vintage buttons in an old Pyrex bowl with a missing lid.
- Roll towels up and store in old baskets, vintage tins, wallpapered boxes, and drawers.

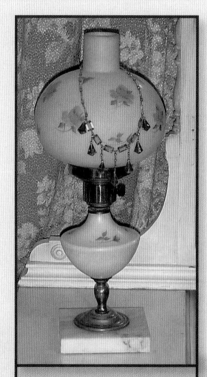

Boudoir lamp, 1930s, glass shaded pink to white, painted roses original, pair, $225.00. Courtesy of www.vintagepastelle.com.

Vintage butlers' cabinet painted white and now used to store a television, $300.00 – 400.00. Courtesy of www.vintagerosecollection.com.

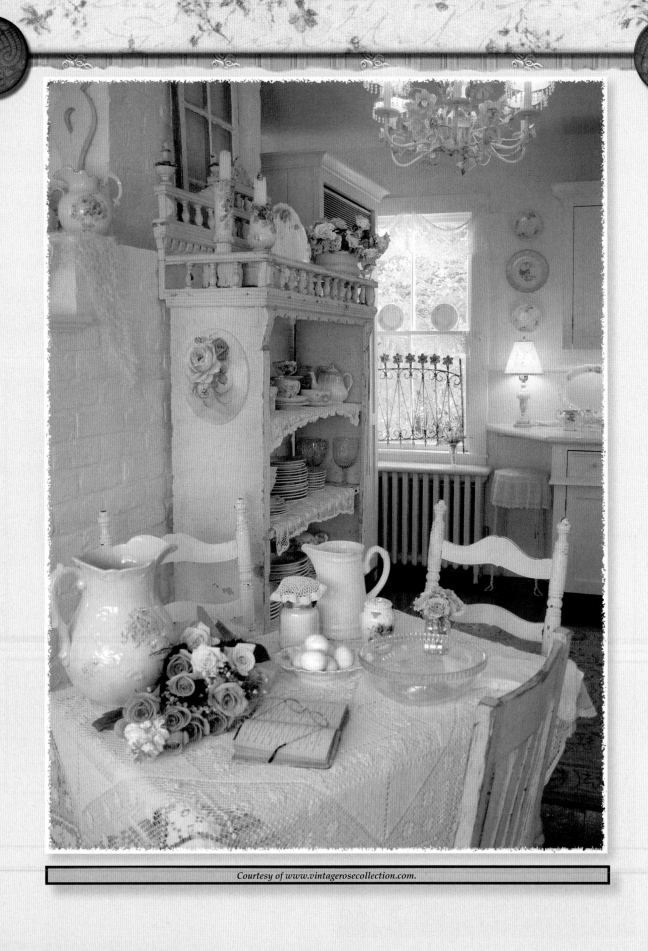

Courtesy of www.vintagerosecollection.com.

Country Cottage Kitchen

All Kinds of Plates
Artist Painted Tole Trays
Baskets & Wicker
Bouquets from the Garden
Canisters & Condiments
Cottage Favorites
Cottage Shabby Accessories
Enamelware: French, German & English
Jars: Glass
Kitchen Chairs
Kitchen Cupboards
Kitchen Tables
Laundry
Wallpaper

Courtesy of www.cottagerags.com.

While there are regional variations to country cottage, there are also many similarities. Country cottages were originally built as simple one room structures to provide protective covering for inhabitants. Early cottages did not have kitchens. Families gathered around an open fire for both warmth and cooking needs. Over the years, one room cottages would be expanded with kitchens, porches, and other modifications which improved cottage living. Because cottages were small, everything the family needed was either mounted on the wall, hung from the ceiling, or cramped on exposed shelves and in open cupboards.

In fact, this busy, jam-packed look is very consistent not only with early cottages but cottage style in general. This is why cottage style is very attractive to loyal collectors. If you are determined to re-create a country cottage feeling you will be on the right track with open shelves, hutches, cupboards, plate racks, wood plank floors, and pine and painted furnishings.

Country cottage kitchen collections include lots of baskets, floral arrangements of dried or fresh flowers in vintage pots or vases, crocks, pottery, mismatched plates, glass storage jars, batter bowls, primitives, old boxes, enamelware, wooden kitchenware, colorful folk décor, and handmade textiles.

Simple painted cottage furniture or primitive or farm style furnishing are typical. Farm animals such as roosters, chickens, and pigs are also common country images as well as cats, hearts, and checkered designs. Window treatments and overstuffed cushions with ruffles are very "country." I have showcased many examples of country cottage favorites in this section.

While many of us think of small simple cottages, there are of course the larger more elaborate cottages that weren't really cottages at all, but summer retreats for wealthy families. Both smaller and grander cottages have inspired prominent designers. For two classic looks think of Ralph Lauren's British country style (jewel tone colors, textured fabrics, and leather furnishings) and Pierre Deux's French county style (small print fabrics, toiles, armoires, palettes of sunny yellow, bright blue, and deep reds). Both these designers continue to influence country cottage trends.

Decorative plates are a perfect addition to a cottage collection. You can create your own wonderful plate collection without resorting to the limited edition themed series plates advertised in magazines. Antique and vintage plates are little pieces of art and history all in one with wonderful workmanship making them ideal for collecting. You can collect by color, motif, shape, size, and texture.

For the cottage collector you would look for unusual feminine designs in pastels with flowers. Floral motifs have been popular on plates for just

about as long as plates have existed. While roses are the most common flower in cottage collecting you could specialize and just collect plates with your favorite flower i.e. tulips or daffodils. On older plates the flowers can be completely hand painted or have hand colored accents which make them extra special.

The "toile" motif with scenic views of the countryside or exotic locales is also ideal for a cottage collection. Toile designs are usually just one color on a solid background. Pink and white or blue and white are typical colors for cottage collecting, but yellow and purple have become very popular lately.

To add interest and variety when collecting plates look for interesting shapes such as square, scalloped, oval, or octagonal.

You can also collect by size. Huge platters or chargers are very dramatic while tiny plates for butter pats are delicate and sweet.

Besides the design applied to the plate such as floral or toile many plates have textured designs in the plates themselves such as basket weaves, scrolls, raised fruit, or roped edges. Look for plates with details like this for extra decorative punch.

Article courtesy of www.DecorativeDishes.net

All Kinds of Plates

The delightful plates shown in this section are part of the lovely collection of Kim Toth-Tevel, owner of www.DecorativeDishes.net

Hand-colored flower basket textured lattice English plate, 8", 1930s, $20.00.

*Colorful hand-painted Italian pottery plate, 9",
1950s, $15.00 – 20.00.*

*Hand-colored floral & scroll English plate, 9",
1930s, $10.00 – 20.00.*

*Antique flow blue scroll with gold accents cake
plate, 7", 1890s, $40.00 – 80.00.*

*Hand-colored floral rope edged octagonal English
plate, 8", 1950s, $10.00 – 20.00.*

Hand-painted floral textured fruit English plate, 6", 1900s, $20.00 – 30.00.

Hand-painted floral textured garland English plate, 9", 1900s, $40.00.

Moss Rose scroll textured edge English plate, 9", 1950s, $30.00.

Classical floral English plate, 6", 1930s, $10.00 – 20.00.

*Hand-colored dramatic floral English plate, 8",
1940s, $20.00 – 30.00.*

*Hand-colored floral octagonal English plate, 8",
1950s, $10.00 – 20.00.*

*Scenic English countryside toile Staffordshire
plate, 10", 1960s, $30.00.*

*Bold floral Staffordshire English plate, 10", 1950s,
$10.00 – 30.00.*

Oriental scenic floral toile Staffordshire English, plate, 6", 1930s, $20.00.

Soft air brush style rose decal American plate, 10", 1950s, $15.00.

Artist Painted Tole Trays

Tole is a French word referring to the decorative art of painting on metalware. Early trays (eighteenth and nineteenth centuries) were called tea boards or tea trays and were painted by a "paintress" using a "one stroke method." These trays were painted black, often with a floral decoration hand painted or stenciled on. This form of decorative art was revived during Colonial times in New England as people often "dressed up" tin ware.

From the 1920s to the 1950s, The Nashco Products Co. of New York City produced numerous hand-painted tea trays in a variety of colors. You will often see colors of Chinese red, black, Wedgwood blue, sage green, cream, and pink in a variety of shapes.

Nashco also produced bowls and vanity trays. Often the artist who painted the tray signed the piece. Nashco has an oval, silver, and black paper label with block lettering. Tole trays are favorite romantic cottage collectibles. Some collectors use their trays and others love to hang them up on a wall creating interesting wall décor.

Prices continue to climb and you will see a full range of values on these items when you are out and about shopping. Condition is everything. Note scratches, paint missing, worn spots, rusting, and warped trays. Most trays I have seen in New England are priced $28.00 – 75.00. As you will see shortly, my

photo contributors indicate an even greater fluctuation in prices of tole trays.

The tole trays which begin this section are from the collection of www.cottagerags.com. Karen, owner of Cottage Rags, sells tole trays in good condition from $45.00 to 95.00 depending on the size, shape, color, and weight of the tray. The trays that follow are from other contributors.

Tole Trays from Other Contributors

Tole tray, hand painted, Chinese red, 6½" x 9½", unmarked, $10.00 – 12.00.
Courtesy of www.nanaluluslinensandhankerchiefs.com.

Tole tray, hand painted, "Nashco," 1930s – 1940s, $25.00 – 45.00.
Courtesy of www.fadedrosecottage.com.

Tole tray, hand painted, Chinese red, 5½" x 7½", 10.00 – 12.00. Courtesy of www.nanaluluslinensandhankerchiefs.com.

Tole Tray, 1940s, hand painted, metal, shabby blue paint, reticulated sides, $95.00 – 125.00. Courtesy of www.romanticroseboutique.com.

Hand-painted tole tray, 1940s, metal, orignal shabby creamy white paint, original floral artwork, round design, $75.00 – 95.00.

Hand-painted aqua tole tray, $45.00 – 95.00. *Courtesy of www. stacysshabbyshoppe.com.*

Baskets & Wicker

White painted basket, reed and wicker, $18.00 – 25.00. *Courtesy of www. fadedrosecottage.com.*

Basket, brown, woven wood and reed, $15.00 – 22.00. *Courtesy of www.fadedrosecottage.com.*

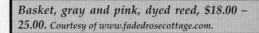

Basket, gray and pink, dyed reed, $18.00 – 25.00. *Courtesy of www.fadedrosecottage.com.*

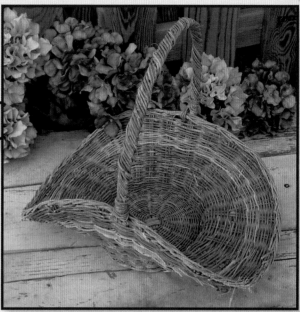

Vintage picnic baskets of varying sizes, $25.00 – 50.00 each. *Courtesy of www.lavenderhillstudio.com.*

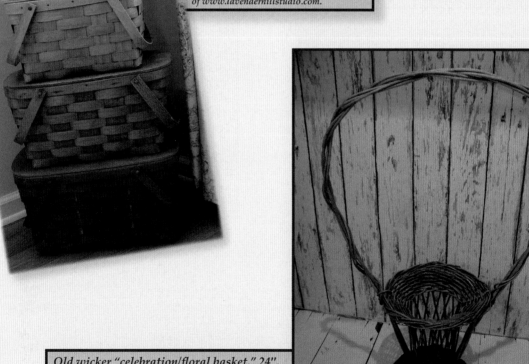

Old wicker "celebration/floral basket," 24", $35.00. *Courtesy of www.teacupsandtwigs.com.*

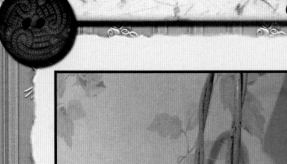

Delicate wicker floral basket, 14", $20.00.
Courtesy of www.teacupsandtwigs.com.

Small antique wicker floral basket, $35.00. Courtesy
of www.teacupsandtwigs.com.

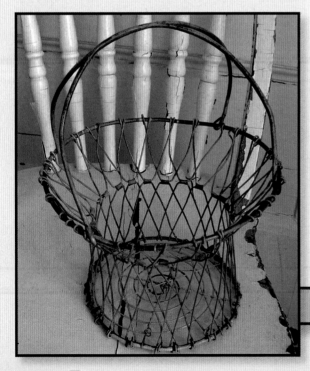

*Bendable basket, wire and plastic, 1900s – 1930s,
$10.00 – 25.00.* Courtesy of www.fadedrosecottage.com.

Large covered basket, reed and wood, 1920s – 1940s,
$18.00 – 25.00. *Courtesy of www.fadedrosecottage.com.*

Fabric lined apple picking basket, wood, wire,
and original fabric, 1900s – 1920s, $35.00 –
40.00. *Courtesy of www.fadedrosecottage.com.*

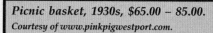

Picnic basket, 1930s, $65.00 – 85.00.
Courtesy of www.pinkpigwestport.com.

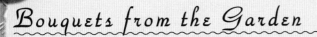

Bouquets from the Garden

One of the characteristic accessories found in cottage homes is fresh or dried flowers in a floral arrangement. Remember many early cottage home owners enjoyed their gardens and it was natural to bring the scents and colors of the outside into the cottage. Today that tradition is maintained. Vintage vases whether it be glass, pottery, hand-painted china, etc. are lovely additions to romantic or country cottage homes.

The vases shown here are all vintage. Prices indicate the bases only. Dried floral arrangements would add $25.00 – 65.00 or more onto the item.

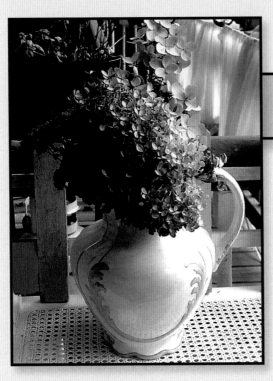

Pitcher, porcelain, marked "Camen," 1890 – 1915, part of six piece set, as shown without matching bowl. $75.00. Courtesy of www.vintagepastelle.com.

Pitcher, tall, porcelain, marked "Camen," 1890 – 1915, part of six piece set, as shown, $95.00 – 125.00. Courtesy of www.vintagepastelle.com.

Aqua deco pottery vase, unmarked, 1930s, $35.00 – 48.00. Courtesy of www.vintagepastelle.com.

Haegar aqua pottery vase, 1930s, $65.00 – 95.00. *Courtesy of www.vintagepastelle.com.*

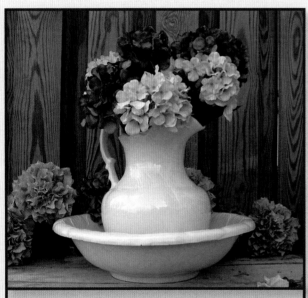

Pitcher and bowl set, white, $85.00 – 125.00. *Courtesy of www.fadedrosecottage.com.*

Vintage silverplate creamer, embellished with vintage china mosaic pieces, artist Penny Carlson of *www.lavendarhillstudio.com,* $35.00 – 55.00

Vintage galvanized watering can, covered in broken vintage china mosaic floral plates, artist Penny Carlson of www.lavenderhillstudio.com, $150.00 $175.00.

Vintage silverplate hotel pitcher covered in broken vintage china plate mosaic transfer-ware, and stained glass, artist Penny Carlson of www.lavenderhill-studio.com, $125.00 – 175.00.

Vintage galvanized watering can, embellished with vintage brown transfer-ware china mosaic pieces, artist Penny Carlson of www.lavenderhillstudio.com, $175.00 – 190.00.

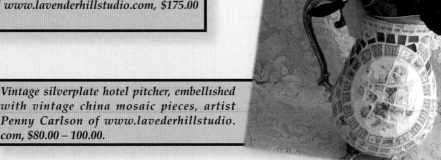

Vintage silverplate hotel pitcher, embellished with vintage china mosaic pieces, artist Penny Carlson of www.lavederhillstudio. com, $80.00 – 100.00.

Canisters & Condiments

Ceramic canisters add a lovely touch to a cottage kitchen and are not only charming but practical, storing sugar, flour, tea, etc. I have included canisters without tops because they too are collectible. Cottage collectors like to use orphaned objects in their kitchens in new ways. Small and large "topless" canisters can be used as planters, containers for odds and ends, and to hold kitchen utensils, pens and pencils, etc.

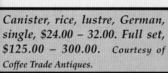

Canister, rice, lustre, German, single, $24.00 – 32.00. Full set, $125.00 – 300.00. Courtesy of Coffee Trade Antiques.

Oil decanter, lustre, German, single, $22.00 – 24.00. Courtesy of Coffee Trade Antiques.

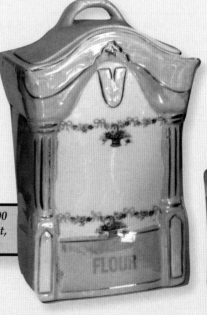

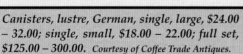

Canisters, lustre, German, single, large, $24.00 – 32.00; single, small, $18.00 – 22.00; full set, $125.00 – 300.00. Courtesy of Coffee Trade Antiques.

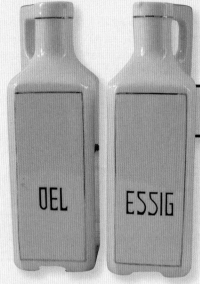

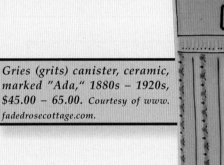

Oil and vinegar bottles, ceramic, German, 1880s – 1920s, $45.00 – 65.00 set. *Courtesy of www.fadedrosecottage.com.*

Gries (grits) canister, ceramic, marked "Ada," 1880s – 1920s, $45.00 – 65.00. *Courtesy of www. fadedrosecottage.com.*

Canister, zimmit (cinnamon), small, single, without top, marked "220," $8.00 – 12.00. *Courtesy of www.fadedrosecottage.com.*

Canisters, zimmit (cinnamon) and nelken (cloves), bottom marked "Dedwig" or "Ledwig," small, singles, no tops, $8.00 – 12.00 each. *Courtesy of www.fadedrosecottage.com.*

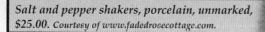

Salt and pepper shakers, porcelain, unmarked, $25.00. *Courtesy of www.fadedrosecottage.com.*

Cottage Favorites

Butter pat, wood, early twentieth century, $10.00 – $15.00. *Courtesy of www.arosewithoutathorn.com.*

Tea crate, English, wood, $40.00 – 50.00. *Courtesy of www.arosewithoutathorn.com.*

Cheese dish, unmarked, English, ironstone, 1880s, $100.00 – 125.00. *Courtesy of www.arosewithoutathorn.com.*

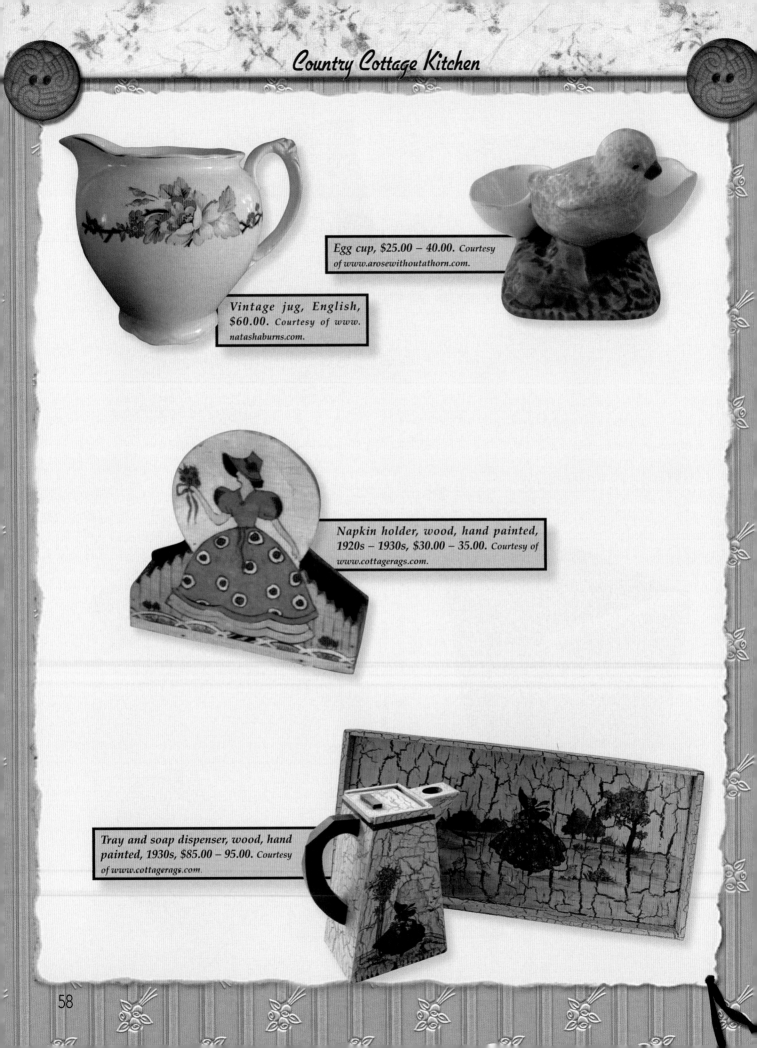

Egg cup, $25.00 – 40.00. *Courtesy of www.arosewithoutathorn.com.*

Vintage jug, English, $60.00. *Courtesy of www.natashaburns.com.*

Napkin holder, wood, hand painted, 1920s – 1930s, $30.00 – 35.00. *Courtesy of www.cottagerags.com.*

Tray and soap dispenser, wood, hand painted, 1930s, $85.00 – 95.00. *Courtesy of www.cottagerags.com.*

Copper teapot, $15.00 – 25.00.
Courtesy of www.fadedrosecottage.com.

Biscuit tin, England, 1930s, $35.00 – 50.00.
Courtesy of www.preservecottage.com.

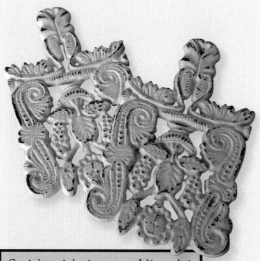

Cast-iron trivets, new white paint,
$12.00 – 22.00 for the pair. *Courtesy
of www.fadedrosecottage.com.*

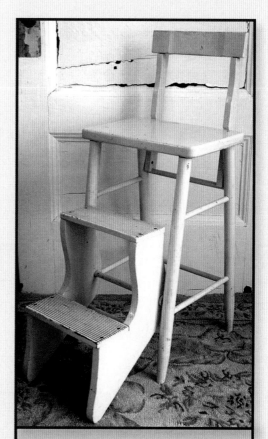

Chippy yellow stepladder and stool, wood
and original paint, 1900s – 1940s, $45.00 –
65.00. *Courtesy of www.fadedrosecottage.com.*

Pink muffin tin, metal and new pink paint, 1920s – 1940s, $12.00 – 15.00. *Courtesy of www.fadedrosecottage.com.*

Metal kitchen scales, 1900s – 1940s, $22.00 – 35.00 each. *Courtesy of www.fadedrosecottage.com.*

Chippy white breadbox, wood and repainted white, $65.00. *Courtesy of www.fadedrosecottage.com.*

Spice cabinet, oak, original decal labels, $125.00. *Courtesy of Coffee Trade Antiques.*

Icebox, porcelain, Majestic, 1800s, $2,000.00 – 3,000.00. *Courtesy of www.pinkpigwestport.com.*

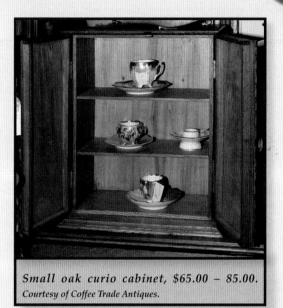

Small oak curio cabinet, $65.00 – 85.00. Courtesy of Coffee Trade Antiques.

Cottage Shabby Accessories

I asked Peggy Jernigan owner of soshabbypink.com to tell me how she got started in painting coffee pots pink? Where did her inspiration to "shabby-tize" everything come from? She explained that as a typical college kid she needed to decorate her apartment in flea market chic because funds were low. Out of necessity she learned how to improvise. She would purchase old and outdated pieces of furniture and décor and then give them a fresh new look with paint, ornamental embellishments, fabric, or wallpaper. After college, however, she "had grown to

love the character and warmth of these items" and continued to decorate her home in the same fashion. She was hooked, she explained. But how did she get to the pink coffee pot stage? Like many shabby artists she just falls in love with odds and ends and dreams about how to transform them into shabby works of art. The household items showcased here are painted with flat unsealed paint making them suitable for decoration and storage of nonfood items only.

All of the pink shabby kitchen accessories shown in this section were created by artist Peggy Jernigan of www.soshabbypink. com.

Old wooden compote, hand-painted white, distressed, and embellished with roses, 28.00 – 35.00.

Old silverplated water pitcher, hand painted, embellished with roses and distressed, $35.00 – 40.00.

Vintage salad set of four, monkey pod wood, hand-painted pink and distressed, decorated with roses, artist Peggy Jernigan of www.soshabbypink. com, $30.00 – 35.00; tall salt shaker shown, single, part of a set, $29.00.

Vintage pot strainer made into decorative wall hanging, painted pink, decorated with roses, distressed, $27.00 – 33.00.

Vintage jelly jars with rose studded vintage metal lids painted by hand and distressed, $35.00 – 39.00.

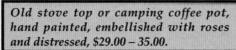

Old stove top or camping coffee pot, hand painted, embellished with roses and distressed, $29.00 – 35.00.

Vintage stove top coffee pot, hand painted, embellished with pink roses and distressed, $29.00 – 35.00.

Vintage electric coffee pot or teapot, hand painted and embellished with roses, distressed, $39.00 – 45.00.

Old aluminum pots in three sizes made into wall décor grouping, painted pink with added pink roses, distressed, $35.00 – 40.00.

Vintage Ball™ tall canning jars, metal one-piece lids painted pink, distressed, and decorated with large roses, $35.00 – 40.00.

Vintage aluminum quart measure, hand painted and distressed, $25.00 – 30.00.

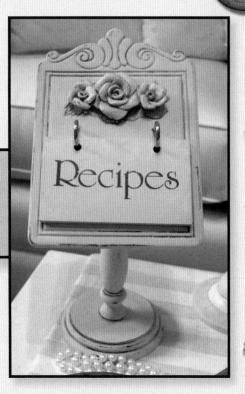

Old kitchen recipe stand, painted pink, antiqued, decorated with pink roses, and distressed, $29.00 – 35.00.

Enamelware: French, German & English

Enamel ware, or granitware as it is also called, was produced by firing a glass-like finish to iron or steel and baking for a long-lasting finish. Enamel ware was often decorated with images from nature and spectacular graphic designs from the Art Nouveau and Art Deco eras. France, England, Germany, Belgium, and Holland produced some of the most collectible and beautiful enamel ware. Old pieces with flowers and animals are some of the most sought after pieces today and can sell for a high premium. The designs were hand painted by true artists and it was looked on as an art form in its own right. Enamel ware that originated from the U.S. was more utiltarian and was devoid of decortation. Early pieces are a lot heavier than later pieces and had several coats of enamel applied to them in various designs including blue swirl, chicken wire, and splatter.

For many years enamelware was an inexpensive collectible, but no longer. Now French enamelware is highly sought after. The more unusual a piece, the more collectible it becomes. There are many items available for beginning collectors such as the more humble plain white mugs, pitchers, refrigerator dishes, plates, and slop buckets. Some of the more collectible

pieces are wash sets such as lavabos (a basin with a water tank above it), utensil racks, match holders, pails, and coffee pots or "biggins" as they are called. This name was given to the three or four part coffee pot that was invented by an Englishman named George Biggin in the eighteenth century. These can be extremely beautiful with spectacular roses, pansies, and birds, and they come in vibrant colors or pastels with gilded accents.

The most popular collectibles are the pieces that were manufactured from the late 1800s to the 1940s. These wonderful old pieces were functional kitchen utensils and appliances in European households and often sustained damage from a lifetime of wear and tear. Areas of damage are to be expected and do not devalue a piece too much unless it is a piece of the decorated image. These early pieces were prone to chips and "craquelure" from being hung from a hook while not in use. They would also have had rivited handles that showed little bumps under the enamel.

A few pieces can be found with their original labels intact and this greatly increases their value and also verifies where it came from. Any antique enamel ware should be washed in hot soapy water. Scouring pads and harsh cleaners should never be used. A gentle buff afterwards with a soft cloth will help your piece last for another 100 years.

Article courtesy of www.arosewithoutathorn.com.

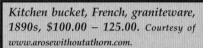

Pitcher and pail, French, granite-ware, Art Deco enamelware, 1920s, $75.00 – 85.00, per piece. Courtesy of www.arosewithoutathorn.com.

Kitchen bucket, French, graniteware, 1890s, $100.00 – 125.00. Courtesy of www.arosewithoutathorn.com.

Pitcher and chamber pot, French, graniteware, enamelware, 1890s, $150.00 – 175.00 each. Courtesy of www.arosewithoutathorn.com.

Lavabo, French, graniteware, enamel-ware, rare yellow color, early twentieth century, $125.00 – 150.00. Courtesy of www. arosewithoutathorn.com.

Pitcher, French, enamelware, large graniteware, early twentieth century, $75.00 – 95.00. Courtesy of www.arosewithoutathorn.com.

Pitcher, French, enamelware, small graniteware, early twentieth century, $100.00 – 125.00. Courtesy of www.arosewithoutathorn.com.

Pitchers, French, enamelware, early twentieth century $75.00 – 175.00 each. Courtesy of www.arosewithoutathorn.com.

Kitchen utensil rack, French, graniteware, 1890s, $150.00 – 175.00. *Courtesy
of www.arosewithoutathorn.com.*

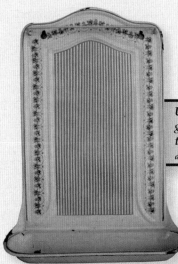

Utensil rack, French, enamelware,
graniteware, early twentieth century, $175.00 – 195.00. *Courtesy of www.
arosewithoutathorn.com.*

Utensil rack with utensils, German,
enamelware, graniteware, early twentieth century, $125.00 – 150.00 for rack;
utensils, $15.00 – 25.00 each. *Courtesy of
www.arosewithoutathorn.com.*

Pitcher, enamelware, 1930s, newly decorated with hand-painted design by artist Cherie Perry, of www.bellarosadesigns.com, $190.00. Courtesy of www.arosewithoutathorn.com.

Pitcher, enamelware, lavender, floral design, $45.00. Courtesy of www.vintagerosecollection.com.

Coffee pot, enamelware, 1940s, $25.00 – 45.00. Courtesy of www.ticklemepink.com.

Teapot, enamel, English enamel, 1900s, $75.00 – 85.00. *Courtesy of www.pinkpigwestport.com.*

Set of German enamelware pots, pans, and utensils, mid twentieth century, pieces individually priced from $55.00 – 300.00 each. Rack is new. *Courtesy of www.bellarosedesigns.com.*

Enamel pitcher, $25.00. *Courtesy of Country Cottage Florist.*

Jars: Glass

Counter jars, vintage Duraglas, new decals, 1940s, $20.00 – 25.00 each. Courtesy of www.pinkpigwestport.com.

Storage jar, original paper label, pure cane sugar, $25.00 – 45.00. Courtesy of Coffee Trade Antiques.

Storage jar, coffee, perhaps part of a Hoosier cabinet, $25.00 – 45.00. Courtesy of Coffee Trade Antiques.

Advertising jar, "Tastee Molasses," $22.00 – 26.00. Courtesy of Coffee Trade Antiques.

Counter jar, red top, pink tinted glass, $35.00 – 45.00. Courtesy of Coffee Trade Antiques.

Candy jars, English, glass, Bakelite and plastic lids, early to mid twentieth century, $45.00 – 75.00 each. Courtesy of www.arosewithoutathorn.com.

Kitchen Chairs

Cottage chair, red, 1900s, $45.00 – 55.00. *Courtesy of www. pinkpigwestport.com.*

Windsor captain's chair, early 1900s, $95.00 – 110.00. *Courtesy of www.pinkpig-westport.com.*

Cottage chair, woven seat, 1900s, $45.00 – 55.00. *Courtesy of www.pinkpigwestport.com.*

Cottage chairs, primitive, early 1900s, $45.00 – 75.00 each. *Courtesy of www.pinkpigwestport.com.*

Kitchen chair, primitive, early 1900s, $35.00 – 50.00. *Courtesy of www.pinkpigwestport. com.*

Kitchen chairs, primitive, peg construction, 1800s, $150.00 – 250.00 pair. *Courtesy of www.pinkpigwestport.com.*

Chair, country ladderback, 1900s, $100.00 – 125.00. *Courtesy of www.pinkpigwestport.com.*

Cottage chair, 1940s, $50.00 – 75.00. *Courtesy of www.pink-pigwestport.com.*

Chair, old green paint, 1940s, $15.00 – 20.00. *Courtesy of www.pinkpigwestport.com.*

Chippy white dinette chair, wood and original paint, 1900s – 1940s, $25.00 – 35.00. Courtesy of www.fadedrosecottage.com.

Kitchen Cupboards

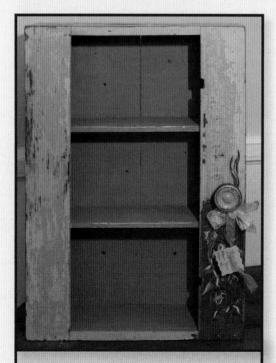

Country cottage open shelf table top, repainted pink and green, $50.00. Courtesy of Country Cottage Florist.

Cupboard, large, white with pink bead board doors, $200.00 – 350.00. *Courtesy of www.freshvintagestyle.com.*

Cupboard, old paint, $250.00 – 300.00. Courtesy of www.preservecottage.com.

Very large cupboard, white, $550.00. Courtesy of www.cottageatleesburg.com.

Old cupboard, beautifully refinished, $250.00 – 275.00. Courtesy of The Bleu Willow.

Kitchen Tables

Enamel/Porcelain Top Tables

Kitchen table, porcelain top, chrome base, 1950s, $75.00 – 95.00. Courtesy of www.pinkpigwestport.com.

Kitchen table, porcelain top, 1930s, $65.00 – 85.00. Courtesy of www.pinkpigwestport.com.

Kitchen table, enamel top, 1930s, $200.00 – 225.00. Chairs, ladderback, set of four, 1900s, $400.00 – 450.00. Courtesy of www.pinkpigwestport.com.

Kitchen table, enamel top, 1920s, $200.00 – 225.00. Courtesy of www.pinkpigwestport.com.

Wood Tables

Kitchen table, wood, painted base, $125.00 – 150.00. Courtesy of www.preservecottage.com.

Oak tavern table, primitive, 1900s, $500.00 – 600.00. Courtesy of www.pinkpigwestport.com.

Farmhouse plank table set, primitive, includes table and four chairs, early 1900s, $600.00 – 800.00. *Courtesy of www. pinkpigwestport.com.*

Trestle table, early, primitive, original paint, 1900s, $500.00 – 600.00. *Courtesy of www.pinkpigwestport.com.*

Work table, primitive, early 1900s, $500.00 – 700.00. *Courtesy of www. pinkpigwestport.com.*

Gateleg table, primitive, early 1900s, $200.00 – 250.00. *Courtesy of www.pinkpigwestport.com.*

Dropleaf Tables

Cottage table set, dropleaf with two chairs, 1940s, $400.00 – 500.00. *Courtesy of www.pinkpigwestport.com.*

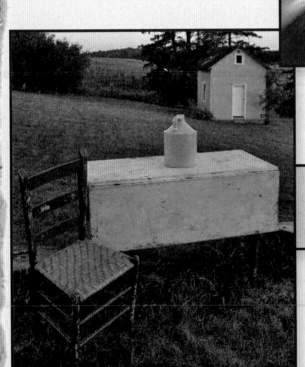

Primitive dropleaf table, late 1800s, $400.00 – 500.00. Cottage chair with vintage fabric, 1930s, $95.00 – 115.00. *Courtesy of www.pinkpigwestport.com.*

Cottage table, painted, Victorian, early 1900s, $300.00 – 400.00. Courtesy of www.pinkpigwestport.com.

Dropleaf table, 1930s, $200.00 – 300.00. Courtesy of www.pinkpigwestport.com.

Laundry

Hamper, basketweave style, painted green, $35.00 – 45.00. Courtesy of Country Cottage Florist.

Basket, chippy blue paint, $15.00 – 18.00. Courtesy of www. freshvintagestyle.com.

Antique window salvaged from a farmhouse in Forestville (Sanilac County), Michigan, artists Ronda Juniper, Ray and Connie Parkinson, $380.00.

Wallpaper

The whimsical novelty vintage wallpaper shown below is courtesy of www.hannastreasures.com. When ordering from Hannah's Treasures, expect to pay about $95.00 – 110.00 a roll with prices rising as the demand for these products are increasing.

Courtesy of www.vintagerosecollection.com.

Romantic Cottage Dining

Chandeliers & Lighting
China Cabinets & Buffets
Cottage Dining Room
Decorative One-of-a-Kind Serving
Decorative Plates
Elegant Touches
Tablecloths, Napkins & Linens
Wallpaper

Courtesy of www.vintagerosecollection.com.

The Victorian era is back in style but kicked up a notch as collectors combine cottage chic with turn of the century elegance. Borrowing design elements from earlier times, the romantic cottage collector enjoys the "feminine" touches that were prevalent during the Victorian period but not the dark and heavy textiles, window treatments, and furniture.

Flowers are everywhere… as patterns on china, tablecloths, napkins, draperies, and wallpaper. Elaborate bouquets of either fresh or dried flowers in attractive vases are always present. Roses are by far the most popular motif for the romantic cottage collector. Hand-painted china, vases, gorgeous serving pieces, collections of decorative plates, figurines,

and candlesticks are all very desired collectibles. Buffets, china cabinets, and dining room sets are painted white or pink and showcase lovely collections of floral teapots, cups and saucers, creamers, pitchers, and other dining accessories. Ornate crystal chandeliers, Italian tole, and decorative sconces are very compatible with divine dining. You will find fine examples of these romantic style collectibles in this section. If you are a true romantic cottage collector you own all of Rachel Ashwell's books on shabby chic and are apt to subscribe to magazines such as *Romantic Country*, *Country Victorian*, and *Romantic Homes*.

Chandeliers & Lighting

Wall sconce, metal, painted, made in Italy, 1940s, single, $65.00 – 85.00. *Courtesy of www. cottagerags.com.*

Candlestick, metal, painted, Italian, 1940s, $35.00 – 45.00. *Courtesy of www.cottgaerags.com.*

Vintage sconce, metal, Italian, once painted brown, repainted pink, green, blue, and lemon, single shown, pair, $120.00 – 150.00. *Courtesy of www.natashaburns.com.*

Chandelier, painted white, vintage Nippon chocolate pot and vintage Limoges cups and saucers added, artist Penny Carlson of www.lavenderhillstudio.com, $495.00 – 525.00.

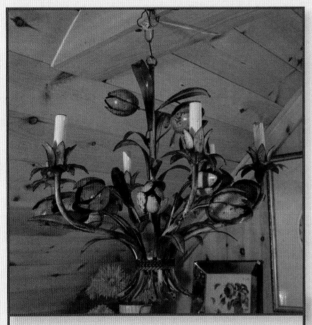

Chandelier, cottage style, metal, flowers, 1930s, $200.00 – 300.00. Courtesy of www.pinkpigwestport.com.

Chandelier, Victorian, brass and crystal, 1800s, $500.00 – 700.00. Courtesy of www.pinkpigwestport.com.

Antique chandelier, Italian crystal, 1930s – 1940s, $500.00 – 1,200.00. *Courtesy of www.stacysshabbyshoppe.com.*

Vintage Italian tole metal daisy 5 arm chandelier, circa 1940, $250.00. *Courtesy of www.vintageprettyandpink.com.*

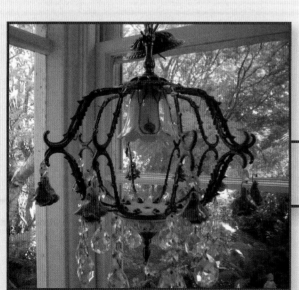

Chandelier, Italian Florentine, capodimonte, roses, and crystals, 1940s, $260.00. *Courtesy of Lesley Hyde of www.vintageprettyandpink.com.*

China Cabinets & Buffets

China cabinet, painted white, distressed, 1930s, $225.00 – 325.00. *Courtesy of www.ticklemepink.com.*

Vintage wall curio, wood, $65.00 – 125.00. *Courtesy of www. bellarosecottage.com.*

China cupboard, painted, 1930s, 150.00 – 175.00. *Courtesy of www. preservecottage.com.*

Cabinet, shabby, $450.00 – 750.00.
Courtesy of www.stacysshabbyshoppe.com.

Vintage ornate server/buffet, repainted white and
ivory, 1940s, $375.00 – 450.00. Courtesy of www.bella-
rosecottage.com.

Vintage server, repainted white and
distressed, 1940s, $325.00 – 375.00.
Courtesy of www.bellarosecottage.com.

China cabinet/hutch, painted white, glass knobs replace original hardware, 1950s, $675.00 – 800.00. *Courtesy of www. bellarosecottage.com.*

Cottage Dining Room

Cottage dining set, painted table, vintage fabric on newly, upholstered chairs, 1940s, $800.00 – 1,100.00. *Courtesy of www.pinkpigwestport.com.*

Vintage drop leaf table with four chairs, painted white, 1950s, $375.00 – 450.00. Courtesy of www.bellarosecottage.com.

Vintage table with four cane-back chairs, painted white, 1950s, $400.00 – 500.00. Courtesy of www.bellarosecottage.com.

Decorative One-of-a Kind Serving

When you are in the antique business you break your share of china plates, teapots, and bowls. For awhile I kept a plastic box of broken pieces in case I would wake up one morning with the irresistible desire to cover a mirror, a table, or lamp base. The urge never materialized so during one of my clean sweep marathon's I threw out the box of broken china. Now I'm finding myself thinking about the broken china again. Perhaps I can learn the craft of broken china mosaics called "pique assiette." This art form was named after Raymond Isidore of Chartres, France, who covered his home both inside and out with broken china in the 1930s. In French, a "pique-assiette" is a scrounger, sponger, or gatecrasher, someone whose interest in stealing a plate would generally be the food on it (www.the-joyofshards.co.uk/index.shtml). Poor Raymond was thought of as being crazy and in French the word for crazy is pique. His home became known as La Maison Picassiette. Some wonder whether picassiette is a pun on Picasso. Despite the early ridicule Raymond Isidore endured, thousands visit La Maison Picassiette each year to see complex and intricate mosaic designs. The term "pique assiette" is widely used around the world. Once considered an "outsider artist," Raymond Isidore has inspired many artists who enjoy working in this form of mosaics.

Carey Chelenza owner of www.dishnchips.com whose work is shown below, taught herself the art of broken china mosaics 10 years ago. She finds the craft quite relaxing and

suggests that beginners read *Making Bits and Pieces Mosaics* by Marlene Hurley Marshall, Storey Publishing. Carey likes to work with colorful china and favors vintage Limoges.

Penny Carlson of lavenderhillstudio.com, another artist featured in this section, uses china shards as well as pieces of stained glass and vintage jewelry. Penny adores covering vintage silver trays, birdhouses, silver teapots, mirrors, and tables.

Many mosaic artists like the challenge of fitting pieces together. For them it is like solving a complex puzzle. The work is very labor intensive and learning the art of cutting the china just right without too much pressure takes lots of practice. So if you are ready to give pique assiette a try, you will need tile adhesive, grout, china, tile nippers, sponges, shop towels, putty knife, grout float, grout sealer, and lots of patience!

Cottage collectors are drawn to vintage collectibles covered in mosaics because they add a whimsical and colorful addition to shabby and romantic décor and table settings. This form of art also brings new life to older treasures and certainly is a way to recycle broken china. The pieces shown in this section can be used as actual serving pieces.

Also shown in this section is the work of Jo-Anne Coletti of vintagerosecollection.com. As you will see throughout this book, Jo-Anne is a very accomplished artist who has mastered the art of painting roses and florals on a variety of vintage objects. Jo-Anne has candidly told me that many of the items she paints on are flea market finds priced quite inexpensively when she first finds them. After she spends hours hand painting these same objects they become one-of-a-kind works of art placing them in an entirely different value category. The same hold true for the mosaics listed below as well.

Vintage mosaic cheese plate with lid, artist Carey Chelenza of www.dishnchips.com, $55.00.

Vintage aluminum tray mosaicked with vintage china, artist Carey Chelenza of www.dishnchips.com, $45.00 – $75.00.

Vintage silverplate tray, embellished with vintage china mosaic pieces, artist Penny Carlson of www. lavenderhillstudio.com, $75.00 – 95.00.

Vintage silverplate tray, embellished with vintage china mosaic pieces, artist Penny Carlson of www.lavenderhillstudio.com, $85.00 – 105.00.

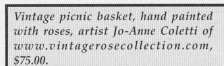

Vintage picnic basket, hand painted with roses, artist Jo-Anne Coletti of www.vintagerosecollection.com, $75.00.

Vintage wood tray, hand painted with roses by artist Jo-Anne Coletti of www.vintagerosecollection.com, $85.00.

Decorative Plates

Transfer-printed cake plate, unmarked, porcelain, 1880s, $35.00 – 45.00.
Courtesy of www.arosewithoutathorn.com.

Transfer-printed cake plate, unmarked, porcelain, 1880s, $35.00 – 45.00.
Courtesy of www.arosewithoutathorn.com.

Transfer-printed cake plate, unmarked, porcelain, 1880s, $35.00 – 45.00. Courtesy of www. arosewithoutathorn.com.

Transfer-printed cake plate, unmarked, porcelain, 1880s, $35.00 – 45.00. Courtesy of www. arosewithoutathorn.com.

Plate, Sevres East Liverpool Potteries, porcelain, transfer printed, 1908, $15.00 – 20.00.
Courtesy of www.arosewithoutathorn.com.

Plate, Grafton China, England, porcelain, transfer printed, early twentieth century, $10.00 – 12.00. Courtesy of www.arosewithoutathorn.com.

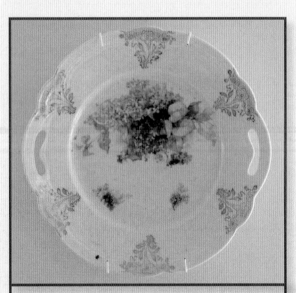

Transfer-printed cake plate, unmarked, porcelain, 1880s, $35.00 – 45.00.
Courtesy of www.arosewithoutathorn.com.

Decorative plate, porcelain, Austria, 1895 – 1945, $25.00 – 55.00.
Courtesy of www.inthepinkantiques.com

Decorative plate, porcelain, ZS&Co. Bavaria, 1895 – 1945, $25.00 – 65.00. Courtesy of www. inthepinkantiques.com.

Cake plate, porcelain, unmarked, 1800s, $25.00 – 75.00. Courtesy of www.inthepinkantiques.com.

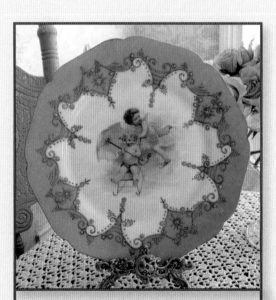

Decorative plate, porcelain, hand-painted Limoges, 1895 – 1935, $35.00 – 125.00. Courtesyof www.inthepinkantiques.com.

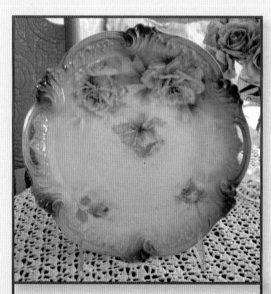

Cake plate, porcelain, RS Prussia, ca. 1895 – 1917, $75.00 – 150.00. Courtesy of inthepinkantiques.com.

Serving plate, porcelain, Sevres China, East Liverpool, Ohio, 1900 – 1908, $25.00 – 55.00. Courtesy of www.inthepinkantiques.com.

Plate, lily design, P.K. Silesia, $24.00 – 30.00. Courtesy of www.stacysshabbyshoppe.com.

Cake plate, porcelain, unmarked, 1845 – 1935, $25.00 – 55.00. Courtesy of www.inthepinkantiques. com.

Plate, rose design, Royal Bavarian, $24.00 – 30.00. Courtesy of www.stacysshabbyshoppe.com.

Platter, floral design, $26.00 – 36.00. Courtesy of www.stacysshabbyshoppe.com.

Decorative plate, $25.00 – 36.00. Courtesy of www.victoriasvintageshoppe.com.

Decorative plate, $25.00 – 36.00. Courtesy of www.victoriasvintageshoppe.com.

Decorative plate, $25.00 – 36.00. Courtesy of www.victoriasvintageshoppe.com.

Elegant Touches

Berry bowl, porcelain, Weimar Germany, 1895 – 1935, $20.00 – 35.00. Courtesy of www.inthepinkantiques.com.

Berry bowl, porcelain, unmarked, 1800s, $15.00 – 35.00. Courtesy of www.inthepinkantiques.com.

Soup bowl, porcelain, Limoges, 1895 – 1945, $25.00 – 55.00. Courtesy of www.inthepinkantiques.com.

Antique berry bowl, porcelain, unmarked, $12.00 – 25.00. Courtesy of www.inthepinkantiques.com.

Berry bowl, porcelain, MZ Austria, 1895 – 1935, $18.00 – 35.00. Courtesy of www.inthepinkantiques.com.

Soup bowl, porcelain, ZS&Co. Bavaria, $25.00 – 55.00. Courtesy of www.inthepinkantiques.com.

Berry bowl, porcelain, RS Germany, 1895 – 1935, $18.00 – 40.00. Courtesy of www.inthepinkantiques.com.

Serving bowl, porcelain, unmarked, ca. 1800 – 1895, $45.00 – 75.00. Courtesy of www.inthepinkantiques.com.

Molded serving bowl, porcelain, unmarked, 1800s, $25.00 – 75.00. Courtesy of www.inthepinkantiques.com.

Molded bowl, porcelain, CT Germany, ca. 1895 – 1935, $75.00 – 150.00. *Courtesy of www. inthepinkantiques.com.*

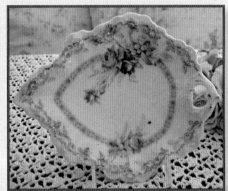

Lemon dish, porcelain, unmarked, $18.00 – 28.00. *Courtesy of www. inthepinkantiques.com.*

Pitcher, porcelain, unmarked, 1800s, $35.00 – 70.00. *Courtesy of www.inthepinkantiques.com.*

Molded serving bowl, porcelain, MZ Austria, 1895 – 1945, $65.00 – 225.00. *Courtesy of www. inthepinkantiques.com.*

Milk pitcher, porcelain, Limoges, hand painted, 1900s, $35.00 – 125.00. *Courtesy of www. inthepinkantiques.com.*

Pitcher, porcelain, unmarked, $45.00 – 95.00. *Courtesy of www. inthepinkantiques.com.*

Footed bowl, porcelain, unmarked, ca. 1800, $65.00 – 150.00. *Courtesy of www. inthepinkantiques.com.*

Lemonade pitcher, porcelain, unmarked, $45.00 – 95.00. *Courtesy of www.inthepinkantiques.com.*

Cream pitcher, porcelain, unmarked, hand painted, $25.00 – 45.00. *Courtesy of www.inthepinkantiques.com.*

Sugar bowl, porcelain, Germany, $25.00 – 45.00. *Courtesy of www.inthepink-antiques.com.*

Antique toothpick holder, porcelain, unmarked, $15.00 – 35.00. *Courtesy of www.inthepinkantiques.com.*

Vase, pedestal, vintage aqua glass, $15.00 – 30.00. *Courtesy of www.inthepinkantiques.com.*

Sugar bowl, porcelain, RS Prussia, ca. 1800, $45.00 – 75.00. *Courtesy of www.inthepinkantiques.com.*

Trivet, porcelain, unmarked, 1800s, $25.00 – 45.00. *Courtesy of www.inthepinkantiques.com.*

Pitcher, salad dressing, aqua glass, $25.00 – 45.00. *Courtesy of www.inthepinkantiques.com.*

Shakers, glass, unmarked, hand painted, $35.00 – 75.00. *Courtesy of www.inthepinkantiques.com.*

Pink rose serving tray, porcelain, MZ Austria, $65.00 – 85.00. *Courtesy of www.fadedrosecottage.com.*

Pink scalloped plate, $18.00; antique sugar shaker, late 1800s, $45.00 – 95.00; pink creamer marked "New Bedford MA," $22.00; rose creamer, $20.00 – 45.00. Courtesy of www.vintagerosecollection.com.

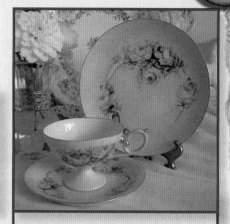

Tea cup, saucer, plate set, aqua and pink roses, Made in Japan, $35.00 – 55.00. Courtesy of www.stacysshabbyshoppe.com.

Biscuit jar, hand painted, Nippon, $150.00. Courtesy of www.stacysshabbyshoppe.com.

Tea cup and saucer, RS Prussia, $35.00. Courtesy of www.stacysshabbyshoppe.com.

Demitasse tea cup set, Austrian roses, $20.00 – 35.00. Courtesy of www.stacysshabbyshoppe.com.

Small teapot, roses, unmarked, $25.00 – 40.00. Courtesy of www.stacysshabbyshoppe.com.

Tea cup and saucer, Colclough, $25.00. Courtesy of www.stacysshabbyshoppe.com.

Tea cup and saucer, $22.00 – 30.00. Courtesy of www.stacysshabbyshoppe.com.

Teacup, porcelain, P.T. Germany, $18.00 – 22.00. Courtesy of www.fadedrosecottage.com.

Rose cottage teacup, porcelain, Royal Dover Fine Bone China, Made in England, $16.00 – 22.00. Courtesy of www.fadedrosecottage.com.

Vintage roses cup and saucer made by Gainsborough, England, $30.00. Courtesy of www.vintageprettandpink.com.

White roses cup, Royal Albert Orleans, $15.00. Courtesy of www.vintageprettyandpink.com.

Large pitcher, "orchid" made by Tunstall England, 1950s, $60.00; medium pitcher, Crown Ducal, England, 1950s, $50.00; small pitcher "midwinter rose," Staffordshire Pottery, England, 1950s, $35.00. Courtesy of www.vintageprettyandpink.com.

Tablecloths, Napkins & Linens

Tablecloths: Printed

Tablecloth, cotton, printed, 1940s – 1950s, $25.00 – 30.00. Courtesy of www.cottagerags.com.

Drapery panel, rayon, printed, 1940s, $65.00 – 85.00.
Courtesy of www.cottagerags.com.

Dishtowel, linen, printed, 1950s – 1960s, $6.00 – 9.00.
Courtesy of www.cottagerags.com

Tablecloth, cotton, printed, 1940s – 1950s, $25.00 – 30.00. Courtesy of www. cottagerags.com.

Tablecloth, cotton damask, pink and white, $35.00. Courtesy of www.cottagerags.com.

Tablecloth, cotton, printed, 1940s – 1950s, $25.00 – 30.00. Courtesy of www.preservecottage.com.

Tablecloth, cross stitch, 1950s, $35.00. Courtesy of www.cottagerags.com.

Romantic Cottage Dining

Tablecloths: White & Sets

Antique white linen and lace 50" square table-cloth and set of six 13" napkins with embroidery and wide filet lace edging, twentieth century, $75. 00. *Courtesy of www.antique-linens.com.*

Napkins, linen, Madera, organdy inserts, embroidered, set of four, $25.00. *Courtesy of www.cottagerags.com.*

Antique white linen tablecloth with embroidered drawn work and crocheted lace edging, nineteenth century, $185.00. *Courtesy of www.antique-linens.com.*

Tablecloth, cotton, drawn work, 1920s, $65.00. *Courtesy of www.cottagerags.com.*

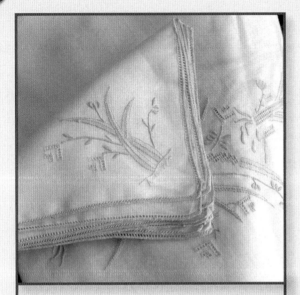

Vintage blue and white linen, shadow work, tea-sized 32" tablecloth and set of four 11" napkins, $45.00. *Courtesy of www.antique-linens.com.*

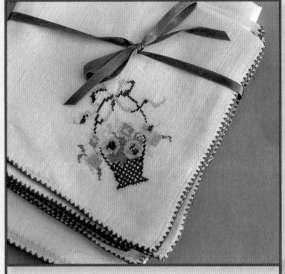

Vintage 10-piece placemat set with five floral embroidered white rice linen placemats and six matching napkins, not all flawless, Chinese, ca. 1930s, $18.00. *Courtesy of www.antique-linens.com.*

Tea Towels

Tea towel, linen and petite point, $20.00 – 22.00. *Courtesy of www.cottagerags.com.*

Tea towel, linen, embroidery, 10.00 – 12.00. *Courtesy of www. cottagerags.com.*

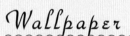
Tea towel, hand embroidered, $12.00 – 15.00. *Courtesy of www.onthecornervintage.com.*

Tea towel, hand embroidered, $12.00 – 15.00. *Courtesy of www.onthecornervintage.com.*

Wallpaper

All of the vintage wallpaper samples shown here are from the 1930s – 1950s and part of the portfolio of hannahstreasure.com. Hannah's Treasures, a vintage wallpaper company, carries a very large catalog of styles, eras, and textures. Owner Marilyn Krehbiel hand picked these lovely cottage prints to show readers the array of classic designs and patterns available. Florals, vibrant botanicals, and soft tone-on-tone stripes are popular patterns. For softer floral designs see the chapter called Sweet Shabby Dreams. Aqua, pink, yellow, lilac, and gray are typical palettes. Marilyn tells me that prices for rolls of wallpaper really vary a great deal, depending on whether you find full rolls or remnants at a flea market, online, in someone's attic, or from a specialty dealer. When ordering form Hannah's Treasures, expect to pay about $95.00 – 110.00 a roll with prices rising as the demand for these products are increasing.

Courtesy of www.vintagerosecollection.com.

Sweet Shabby Dreams

Bed Benches
Beds: Full
Beds: Headboards & Footboards
Cabinets
Dressers: White & Pastel
Lamps
Pillow Cases
Shabby Night Tables
Textiles, Quilts & Blankets
Wall Décor: Florals
Wallpaper

Courtesy of www.arosewithoutathorn.com

here is an entire "cottage industry" out there of cottage collectors and sellers who adore Shabby Chic type collectibles made popular by creator Rachel Ashwell. Her company was founded in 1989 in Santa Monica, California, offering her signature slip covered furniture and flea market finds. In 1996, her first book *Shabby Chic* was released and had women everywhere copying her style. Misfit pieces, new uses for old furniture, faded fabrics, rusted metal side tables, unusual headboards, chippy painted nightstands, and lots of white textiles with soft floral accents are all very shabby. Three more books followed her first and her brand grew into company stores worldwide. Shabby Chic has not only influenced women everywhere but has completely shaken up the interior design industry. It is as if Rachel Ashwell has given permission to all of us to experiment with home décor. If Rachel could use an old iron gate as a headboard, others could take apart a funky picket fence or chippy painted barn door and create their own shabby headboards. In this section you will find many furnishings and bedroom accessories inspired by Rachel Ashwell's successful Shabby Chic brand as well as other vintage finds which are suitable for cottage style interiors.

Bed Benches

Cottage settee made from antique iron baby crib, $150.00 – 225.00.
Courtesy of www.inthepinkantiques.com.

Child's bench w/footstool, 1940s, oak bed headboard, repainted cottage green, new rose fabric cushions and covered footstool, $245.00 – 295.00.
Courtesy of www.romanticroseboutique.com.

Vintage bed bench, made out of a full bed, hand-painted roses, painted and waxed, 1950s, $425.00 – 500.00. *Courtesy of www.bellarosecottage.com.*

Vintage bed bench, made out of a full vintage rope bed, painted white, early 1900s, $400.00 – 475.00. *Courtesy of www.bellarosecottage.com.*

Vintage bed bench, made from a 1940s bed, painted white and distressed, $400.00 – 500.00. *Courtesy of www.bellarosecottage.com.*

Beds: Full

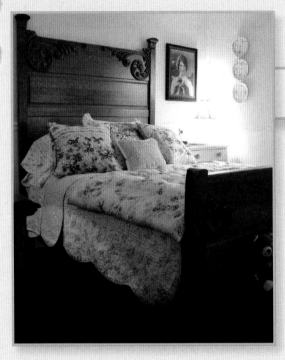

Bed, oak, American, 1880s, $1,250.00 – 1,500.00. Courtesy of *www.arosewithoutathorn.com.*

Antique iron bed, French, 1920s, $700.00 – 800.00. Courtesy of *www.pinkpigwestport.com.*

Antique iron bed, painted, 1940s, $300.00 – 500.00. Courtesy of www. pinkpigwestport.com.

Vintage folding camp bed, 1940s, $300.00 – 400.00. Courtesy of www. pinkpigwestport.com.

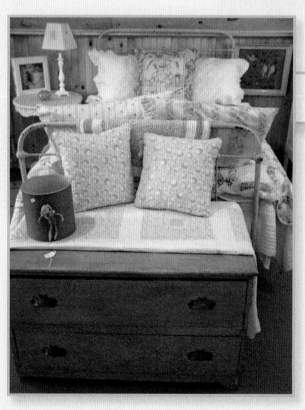

Antique full bed, cottage chic, 1940s, $700.00 – 800.00. Courtesy of www.pinkpigwestport.com.

Pet beds, made of pine and bead board with recycled antique adornments, $300.00. Courtesy of www. countrycottagechic.com.

Beds: Headboards & Footboards

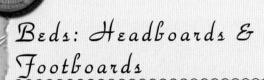

Vintage, solid wood head/ footboard, wonderful details, still has the original wheels on both pieces, painted linen white and distressed just enough, $275.00. Courtesy of www. countrycottagechic.com.

Spindle bed, solid wood, vintage twin head and foot board, painted linen white and distressed, $275.00. Courtesy of www. countrycottagechic.com.

Vintage full bed, painted pink, 1940s, $375.00 – 475.00. Courtesy of www.bellarosecottage.com

Vintage full size bed, painted white, appliqués added to headboard and footboard, mid 1900s, $350.00 – 425.00. *Courtesy of www.bellarosecottage.com.*

Cabinets

Victorian record cabinet, painted white, record player removed, used to store towels, $300.00 – 400.00. *Courtesy of www.vintagerosecollection.com.*

Vintage butler's cabinet, painted white and now used to store a television, $300.00 – 400.00. *Courtesy of www. vintagerosecollection.com.*

Dressers: White & Pastels

Cottage style dresser, painted, 1930s, $200.00 – 350.00. Courtesy of www.pinkpigwestport.com.

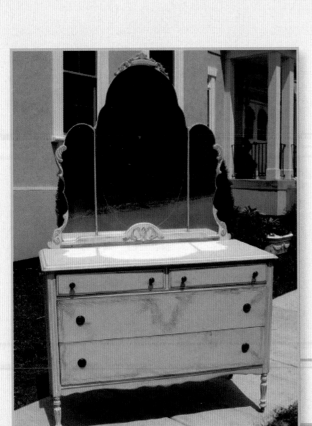

Cottage linen chest with mirror, 1930s, $400.00 – 475.00. Courtesy of www.pinkpigwestport.com.

Vintage dresser with tiara mirror, 1930s, painted pink and distressed, $400.00 – 450.00. Courtesy of www.bellarosecottage.com.

Vintage dresser with mirror, 1940s, painted ivory and distressed, appliqués added, $395.00 – 450.00. Courtesy of www.bellarosecoattage.com.

Vintage chest, 1930s, painted ivory and distressed, appliqués and glass knobs added, $400.00 – 475.00. Courtesy of www.bellarosecottage.com.

Lamps

Lamp, metal base and glass shade, Depression era, 1930s, excellent condition, $75.00 – 100.00. Courtesy of www.arosewithoutathorn.com.

Lamp, hand-crafted, silverplated vintage teapot transformed into a lamp by www.dishnchips.com, $75.00 – 150.00.

Lamp, hand-crafted, vintage cup and saucer sets, English, created into a table lamp by www.dishnchips.com. $150.00.

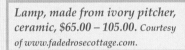

Lamp, made from ivory pitcher, ceramic, $65.00 – 105.00. *Courtesy of www.fadedrosecottage.com.*

Lamps, ceramic, replaced shades, missing cord on one lamp, pair, $45.00 – 65.00.

Vintage silverplate sugar bowl turned into a lamp, embellished with vintage china mosaic pieces, artist Penny Carlson of www.lavendarhillstudio. com, $70.00 – 80.00.

Vintage silverplated teapot turned into a lamp, embellished with vintage china mosaic pieces, artist Penny Carlson of www.lavendarhillstudio.com. $185.00 – 195.00.

Vanity lamps, glass, pair, $35.00 – 40.00. *Courtesy of www.preservecottage.com.*

Pillow Cases

Pillow case, feedsack, cotton, mid twentieth century, $50.00 – 75.00. Courtesy of www.arosewithoutathorn.com.

Pillowcase, handmade, cotton, crochet, mid twentieth century, $25.00 – 35.00. Courtesy of www. arosewithoutathorn.com.

Pillowcases, Fruit of the Loom, cotton, mid twentieth century, $50.00 – 75.00. Courtesy of www.arosewithoutathorn.com.

Pillowcases, cotton, mid twentieth century, $25.00 – 35.00. Courtesy of www.arosewithoutathorn.com.

Pillowcases, cotton, floral, pair, $25.00 – 28.00. Courtesy of www.preservecottage.com.

Shabby Night Tables

Humidor/magazine stand, old paint, 1920s – 1930s, $50.00 – 70.00. Courtesy of www.preservecottage.com.

Table, painted, Duncan Phyfe, 1940s, $75.00 – 95.00. Courtesy of www.pinkpigwetport.com.

End table, painted white, 1940s, $125.00 – 200.00. *Courtesy of www. pinkpigwestport.com.*

Pair of French Provincial nightstands, painted pink and white, original hardware, 1960s, $300.00 – 350.00. *Courtesy of www.bellarosecottage.com.*

Vintage stand with drawers, painted a soft pink, original hardware, 1950s, $275.00 – 350.00. *Courtesy of www.bellarosecottage.com.*

Vintage pair of nightstands, painted white, original hardware, 1940s, $300.00 – 375.00. *Courtesy of www.bellarosecottage.com.*

Vintage pair of nightstands, painted white with soft pink, original hardware, 1950s, $300.00 – 375.00. *Courtesy of www.bellarosecottage.com.*

Textiles, Quilts & Blankets

Quilt, appliqúe basket and flowers, cotton, 1920s, $150.00 – 200.00. *Courtesy of www.cottagerags.com.*

Quilt, cotton, 1930s, $395.00 – 450.00.
Courtesy of www.cottagerags.com.

Quilt, Texas Lonestar, cotton,
1920s – 1930s, $295.00 – 350.00.
Courtesy of www.cottagerags.com.

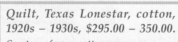

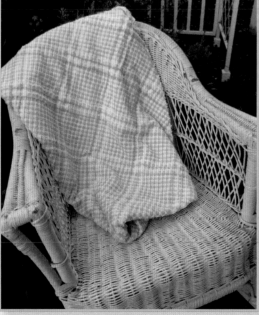

Chenille bedspread, cotton, 1940s, $65.00
– 75.00. Courtesy of www.cottagerags.com.

Quilt, Double Wedding Ring, cotton, 1920s – 1930s, $395.00 – 450.00. *Courtesy of www.cottagerags.com.*

Chenille bedspread, cotton, 1940s, $95.00 – 125.00. *Courtesy of www.cottagerags.com.*

Quilt, small, 1930s, $100.00. *Courtesy of www. ntashaburns.com.*

Bedspread, cotton chenille, double, 1940s, $55.00 – 65.00. *Courtesy of www. preservecottage.com.*

Bedspread, vintage chenille, 1940s, $200.00 – 300.00. *Courtesy of www.pinkpigwestport.com.*

Bedspread, cotton chenille, double, 1940s, $55.00 – 65.00. *Courtesy of www.preservecottage.com.*

Wall Décor: Florals

Needlepoint, framed, pair, $25.00 – 45.00. *Courtesy of www.cestchouettehome.com.*

Original ceiling tin frame, floral print, $125.00. *Courtesy of www.ticklemepinkboutique.com.*

Victorian yard long print, $125.00. *Courtesy of Coffee Trade Antiques.*

Three-diminsional pic-
ture, 1940s, $25.00. Courtesy
of Coffee Trade Antiques.

Floral print,
framed, $25.00.
Courtesy of Coffee
Trade Antiques.

Oilette, made to look
like oil painting, $24.00.
Courtesy of Coffee Trade
Antiques.

Antique wood frame, 1900
– 1920, new rose print,
$25.00 – $65.00. Courtesy of
www.ticklemepinkboutique.com.

Emma Rose canvas print framed in old pink molding by artist Jo-Anne Coletti, $49.00.

Original oil painting of roses with antique frame, by artist Jo-Anne Coletti, $225.00.

Wallpaper

Values: See page 80 for information on vintage wallpaper.

Courtesy of www.arosewithoutathorn.com.

Rock-a-Bye Cottage Baby

Baby Quilts
Child Chairs
Dolls
Doll Furniture
Doll Houses
Hand Embroidered Linens
Nursery Accessories
Nursery Pillows
Playtime
Wall Décor: Chromo Lithographs
Wallpaper

Courtesy of www.pinkpigwestport.com.

The nursery is a perfect place to bring in cottage style furnishings and décor. Starting with the basics, older painted dressers, tables, and beds, painted in soft pastels are an affordable way to equip a darling baby's room. Dressers can be converted into a changing table with just a little ingenuity. Old wardrobes are idea for hanging tot-sized clothing. Perhaps you are interested in a more whimsical nursery. You might consider purchasing an old cupboard and painting it in bold colors. These practical furnishings have lots of shelf space and storage room.

Adding vintage accessories such as child-sized rockers, chairs and tables, doll houses, and vintage toys make charming and interesting additions to a cottage style nursery. Miniature doll-sized dressers can be hung on a wall and used as a cute shelf.

Be creative, not only can you use your wall space for collections, but consider hanging vintage collectibles from the ceiling or on a line. A clothes line hung across a corner area looks adorable with colorful children's hankies, vintage birthday cards, 1940s and 1950s mittens, embroidered linens with children's themes, toy airplanes, etc.

Vintage textiles are the cat's meow in a rock-a-way cottage baby nursery. Use vintage fabric to make crib bumpers or pillows. Chenille or patchwork quilts are favorites in vintage nurseries. Look for yellowing, holes, thinned areas, worn areas, etc. But if you find an old quilt that is damaged, don't be so quick to discard it, it can be used to make doll covers, stuffed animals, pillows, etc.

I have included a beautiful collection of sweet wallpaper in this section. As discussed earlier in this book, you can use children's wallpaper in many ways besides wall coverings. These adorable patterns make great lining for drawers and shelves as well as terrific artwork when framed.

For more information about using vintage finds in a baby's room, be sure to review the bibliography at the end of the book.

Baby Quilts

Baby chenille blanket, pink floral, cotton, 1940s, $40.00 – 45.00. Courtesy of www.cottagerags.com.

Baby blanket, bunnies tumbling, cotton, cross-stitch, 1950 – 1960, $35.00 – 40.00. Courtesy of www.cottagerags. com.

Baby blanket, Noah's Arc, cotton, cross-stitch, 1950 – 1960, $50.00 – 60.00. *Courtesy of www.cottagerags.com.*

Baby chenille blanket, bunnies, cotton, 1940s, $35.00 – 40.00. *Courtesy of www.cottagerags.com.*

Baby chenille blanket, cat in overalls, cotton, 1940s, $25.00 – 30.00. *Courtesy of www.cottagerags.com.*

Baby chenille blanket, Scottie dog, cotton, 1940s, $40.00 – 45.00. Courtesy of www.cottagerags.com.

Quilt, chenille, window pane, 1930s – 1940s, 66" l x 44" w, $32.00. Courtesy of www.sweetyesterdays.com.

Children's Chairs

Child's chair, handmade, old paint, 1930s – 1940s, $35.00 – 40.00. Courtesy of www.preservecottage.com.

Child's chair, primitive, $65.00 – 75.00. Courtesy of www.pinkpigwestport.com.

Child's chair, red painted, $45.00 – 65.00. Courtesy of www.cottageatleesburg.com.

Child's chair, chippy paint, $30.00. Courtesy of The Bleu Willow.

Child's cottage chair, chippy white paint, $45.00. Courtesy of Country Cottage Florist.

Youth rocker, late 1800s, $150.00 – 250.00. Courtesy of www. pinkpigwestport. com.

Child's table set, painted, 1930s, $200.00 – 300.00. *Courtesy of www.pinkpigwestport.com.*

Dolls

Boy doll, Dean's of England, felt body and papier mache head with hand-painted features, mid twentieth century, good condition, $125.00 – 175.00. Girl doll, cloth body, original clothes, hand-painted face, 1920s, fair condition, $200.00 – 300.00. *Courtesy of www. arosewithoutathorn.com.*

Doll, cloth body, black Americana with original clothes, good condition, $55.00 – 75.00. *Courtesy of www. arosewithoutathorn.com.*

Truck, Marx, tin litho, farmyard decals, very good condition, $100.00 – 150.00. Andy rag-doll, cloth, homemade, mid twentieth century, fair condition, $55.00 – 95.00. *Courtesy of www. arosewithoutathorn.com.*

Doll, plastic face, 1940s, $58.00. Courtesy of The Bleu Willow.

Doll Furniture

Doll bed/crib, 1940s, pine, original shabby white paint, wooden rollers, bed cushion from antique quilt, $95.00 – 125.00. Courtesy of www.romanticroseboutique.com.

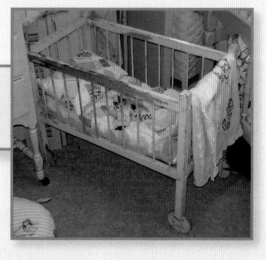

Vintage doll bed, painted white, embellished with vintage china mosaic pieces, artist Penny Carlson of www.lavenderhillstudio.com, $175.00 – 195.00.

Vintage drop leaf end table, painted white, embellished with vintage china mosaic pieces, artist Penny Carlson of www.lavenderhillstudio. com, $999.00 – 1,200.00.

Stroller, loom,1920s, $275.00 – 375.00. Courtesy of www.pinkpigwestport.com.

Doll crib, wooden, decal trim, 1930s, $125.00 – 200.00. Courtesy of www.pinkpigwestport.com.

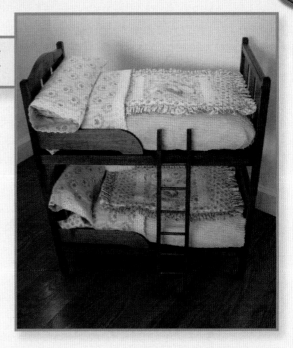

Doll bunk beds, $125.00 – 150.00. With custom bedding, add $150.00. Courtesy of www.arosewithoutathorn.com.

Doll crib, $50.00 – 150.00. With custom bedding add $100.00. Courtesy of www.arosewithoutathorn.com.

Doll Houses

Dollhouse mansion, Marx, tin lithograph, 1950s, excellent condition, $250.00 – 350.00. Courtesy of www.arosewithoutathorn.com.

Upper image: Dollhouse mansion, Marx, tin lithograph, 1950s, excellent condition, $250.00 – 350.00. Lower image: Dollhouse, Marx, tin lithograph, 1950s, excellent condition, $45.00 – 65.00. When found with original furniture add $50.00 – 100.00.

Hand-embroidered Linens

Embroidered baby bib, 1950s – 1960s, $8.00 – 12.00. Courtesy of www.primsrosedesign.com.

Embroidered baby bib, 1950s – 1960s, $8.00 – 12.00. Courtesy of www.primrosedesign.com.

Nursery Accessories

Doctor's baby scale, wicker and metal, rare baby decal, early twentieth century, excellent condition, $125.00 – 175.00. Courtesy of www.arosewithoutathorn.com.

Nursery storage set, plastic, hand painted, 1940s, excellent condition, $25.00 – 45.00. *Courtesy of www.arosewithoutathorn.com.*

Child's potty, enamel, 1940s, $26.00 – 30.00. *Courtesy of www.cottagerags.com.*

Child's cup, pottery, Hankscraft, 1930s – 1940s, $22.00 – 28.00. *Courtesy of www.cottagerags.com.*

Laundry baby hoop, wood, minus original bag, hand painted, 1940s, excellent condition, $65.00 – 85.00. *Courtesy of www.arosewithoutathorn.com.*

Hanger, child's, with decal trim, early 1900s, $45.00 – 65.00. *Courtesy of www.pinkpigwestport.com.*

Light switch, plastic, 1940s, $40.00 – 45.00. Courtesy of www. cottagerags.com.

Captain's chair, 1940s, oak, re-painted cottage white, hand painted pink roses, $125.00 – 145.00. Courtesy of www.romanticroseboutique.com.

Nursery Pillows

Pillow, hooked, cotton, 1940s, $40.00 – 45.00. Courtesy of www.cottagerags.com.

Pillow, cotton, tinted, embroidery, Vogart, 1940s, $25.00 – 30.00. Courtesy of www.cottagerags.com.

Pillow, cotton, tinted, embroidery, Vogart, 1940s, $25.00 – 30.00. Courtesy of www.cottagerags.com.

Pillow, cotton, tinted, embroidery, Vogart, 1940s, $20.00 – 25.00. *Courtesy of www.cottagerags.com.*

Pillow, cotton huck, tinted, embroidery, 1950s, $15.00 – 20.00. *Courtesy of www.cottagerags.com.*

Pillow, cotton, pieced, Around the World pattern, 1930s, $25.00 – 30.00. *Courtesy of www.cottagerags.com.*

Playtime

Toy trunk, wood, rare circus decals, mid twentieth century, excellent condition, $125.00 – 200.00. Courtesy of www. arosewithoutathorn.com.

Doll suitcase, cardboard, 1940s, $24.00 – 28.00. Courtesy of www.cottagerags.com.

Book, Chatterwell Stories, 1911, $35.00 – 45.00. Courtesy of www.fadedrosecottage.com.

Chalkboard and cut out's, late 1940s, $50.00 – 65.00. Courtesy of www.pinkpigwestport.com.

Vintage child's chalkboard, 1940s, $95.00 125.00. Courtesy of www.pinkpigwestport.com.

Wall Décor: Chromo Lithographs

These vintage prints are courtesy of www.arosewithoutathorn. com ranging from the late 1880s to the 1940s. Many were intended for calender use and would be printed with the name of a business. This is very helpful in dating a piece. The prices range from an inexpensive $10.00 all the way up to $100.00 plus. Anything that includes a dog is usually more collectible and will sell for considerable more.

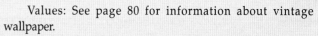

Wallpaper

Values: See page 80 for information about vintage wallpaper.

PUT TOYS AWAY

HANG UP TOWELS

SHOES IN PLACE

USE YOUR WASHCLOTH

DRINK YOUR MILK

HANG UP CLOTHES

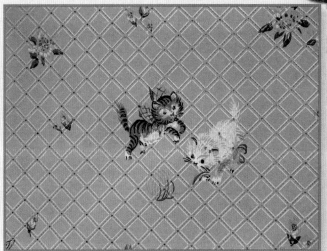

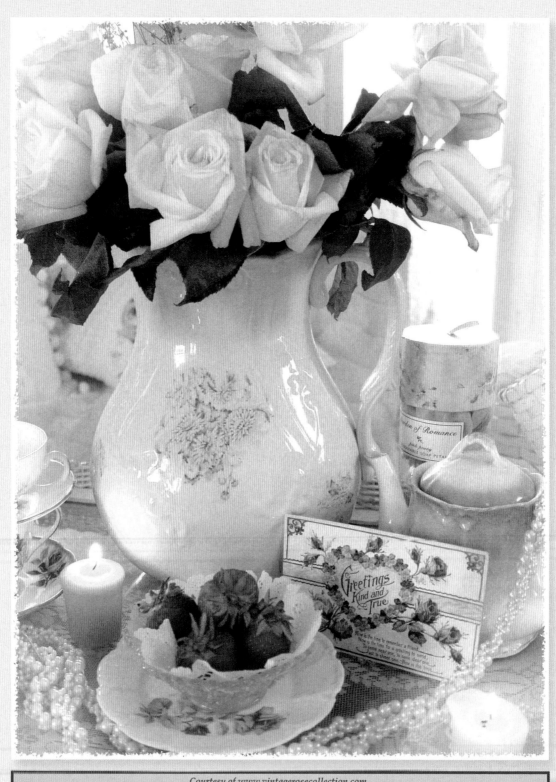

Pretty in Print

Accessories: Shabby Cubbies
Desks
Keepsake Boxes
Postcards
Romance Novels
Valentines
Vintage Images: Chromo Lithographs
Vintage Images: Pretty Women

Courtesy of www.vintagerosecollection.com.

efore computers and cell phones, the properly mannered woman sat at her writing desk and quietly penned a beautiful letter or postcard to a loved one or enjoyed reading a romantic novel. Written correspondence was so very important and often took place in a designated room such as the sitting room or den. From this era you will find so many gorgeous postcards and vintage paper which can be saved in a collection or framed and used as wall décor.

Other keepsakes which are popular to collectors who are charmed by pretty images are prints from calendars and valentines. Valentines from the 1940s – 1950s are easy to find and reasonable priced. Victorian era valentines are in a totally different category and can run as high as buying a good vintage print. A very hot item to keep your eyes open for are books with pretty cover images of women with hats or other portrait images as well as older romance novels. These sought after books keep climbing in price and are usually around $20.00 – 26.00.

Whether you are interested in collecting ephemera (vintage paper) or you are ready to transform one of your rooms into an office, you will find that cottage style affords you great flexibility in collecting options.

Today, many are charmed by the look and feel of a sitting room inspired by the Victorian era but updated with modern conveniences. You can have the best of both worlds. The sitting room or office area is lovely with romantic country touches. Mixing darker woods with chippy painted furniture is so cottage-y. Writing desks are beautiful vintage heirlooms which are not only decorative but so functional to organize mail and office needs. If you find a desk in oak or darker woods, lighten the look by painting it white or a soft green. You can wallpaper the inside cubbies or line drawers with pretty fabric. Accompanying your desk use lots of feminine accessories such as florals, small picture frames, lace doilies, soft fabrics, flower arrangements, hand-painted pastel and white palettes, vanity lamps, etc.

Accessories: Shabby Cubbies

Vintage cubby, original old white paint, $150.00. Courtesy of www.vintagerosecollection.com.

Magazine caddy, painted green, distressed, $45.00 – 65.00. Courtesy of www.ticklemepinkboutique.com.

Bookend, metal, hand painted, 1940s, single, $28.00 – 32.00. Courtesy of www.cottagerags.com.

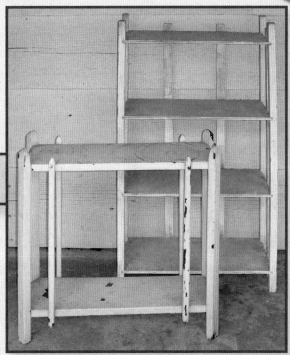

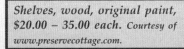
Shelves, wood, original paint,
$20.00 – 35.00 each. *Courtesy of www.preservecottage.com.*

Shabby paper sorter, pink and blue, $20.00. Courtesy of *www.freshvintagestyle.com.*

File box, older, wooden, dovetailed desk, painted and distressed, decorated with roses, $39.00 – 45.00. *Courtesy of www.soshabbypink.com.*

Pretty in Print

Desks

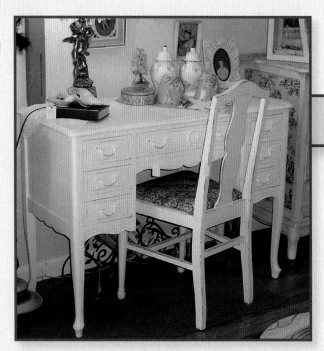

Desk, vintage, repainted white, distressed, $225.00 – 325.00. Courtesy of www.ticklemepinkboutique.com.

Desk, wood, $250.00 – 500.00. Courtesy of www.inthepinkantiques.com.

Antique lady's desk, hand painted black with pink roses, artist Jo-Anne Coletti of www.vintagerosecollection.com, original price of desk, $95.00, with art work, $295.00

Keepsake Boxes

The keepsake boxes shown here are courtesy of The Coffee Trade Antiques. They sell for $18.00 – 28.00.

Postcards

These beautiful vintage floral postcards are from the collection of ticklemepinkboutique.com. Values would range from $3.00 – 8.00 each depending on age, condition, and rarity.

Birthday Greetings!

A Joyful, Happy Easter-tide.

Many Happy Returns.

Heartiest Congratulations.

In pleasure's dream, or
sorrows hour,
In crowded hall or lonely
bower,
The business of my soul
shall be
For ever to remember thee.

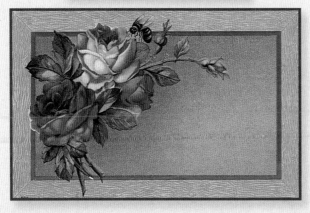

Best Wishes

This Greeting true
I send to you—
May all your life
Be free from strife—
And Happiness attend you

Birthday Greetings.

BIRTHDAY
GREETINGS

Blanche Catherman.

Many Happy Returns of the Day.

Very Best Wishes

Golden
Days
Be
Thine

BEST
WISHES

BIRTHDAY
GREETINGS

Sannie

TO MY
VALENTINE

I send thee Poppies red.
For I've often heard it said.
That if you breathe its
perfume deep,
'Twill cast o'er you
sweet sleep
And perchance you'll
dream in time.
That you will be my
Valentine.

Roses
Sweet
And warm regard.
These I send you with
This Card:
They shall bear Assurance true.
That your Friend remembers you.

Romance Novels

Romance novel, Rachel Cade, Charles Mercer, original dust jacket, 1956, very good condition, $10.00 – 20.00. *Courtesy of www.arosewithoutathorn.com.*

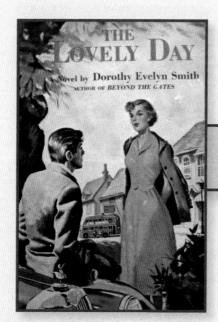

Romance novel, The Lovely Day, Dorothy Evelyn Smith, original dust jacket, 1957, good condition, $8.00 – 15.00. *Courtesy of www.arosewithoutathorn.com.*

Romance novel, Bugles in Her Heart, Lida Larrimore, original dust jacket, 1944, good condition, $8.00 – 15.00. *Courtesy of www.arosewithoutathorn.com.*

Romance novel, Tarpaper Palace, *Lida Larrimore*, original dust jacket, 1942, fair condition, $8.00 – 10.00. *Courtesy of www.arosewithoutathorn.com.*

Romance novel, Beyond Tomorrow, *Lida Larrimore, original dust jacket, 1941, good condition, $10.00 – 15.00. Courtesy of www.arosewithoutathorn.com.*

Romance novel, Don't You Cry For Me, *Mary Freels Rosborough*, original dust jacket, 1957, excellent condition, $10.00 – 20.00. *Courtesy of www. arosewithoutathorn.com.*

Valentines

The charming valentines shown here are from the collection of www.primrosedesign.com and would sell for $4.00 – 6.00. each.

Somebody loves you
      Deep and true
If I wasn't bashful
      I'd tell you who

TELL ME "WEATHER" I STILL "RAIN"
IN YOUR HEART MY VALENTINE

JUST PEDDLING MY WAY

Valentine Greetings

Vintage Images: Chromo-Lithographs

Print, chromolithograph, 1940s, mint condition $50.00 – 75.00. Courtesy of www.arosewithoutthorn.com.

Print, chromolithograph, printed in Germany, early twentieth century, mint condition, $50.00 – 75.00. Courtesy of www.arosewithoutathorn.com.

Print, Zoe Mozart, chromolithograph, early twentieth century, mint condition, $35.00 – 50.00. Courtesy of www.arosewothoutathorn.com.

Print, chromolithograph, printed in Germany, early twentieth century, mint condition, $50.00 – 75.00. Courtesy of www.arosewitoutathorn.com.

Vintage Images: Pretty Women

These beautiful vintage floral postcards are from the collection of www.ticklemepinkboutique.com. Values would range from $3.00 – 8.00 each depending on age, condition, and rarity.

HEUREUSE FÊTE

The chestnut is said to
bring luck in the fall,
But Good Luck the year round
is no "chestnut" at all.

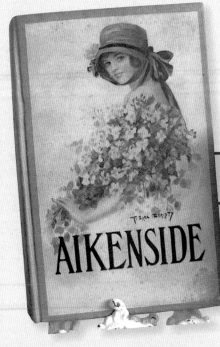

AIKENSIDE

Antique novel, pretty lady
cover, Aikenside, $22.00
– 25.00.

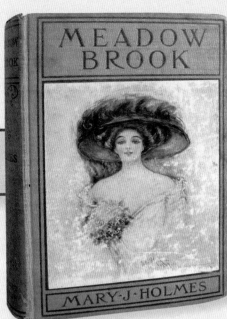

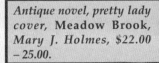

Antique novel, pretty lady cover, **Meadow Brook, Mary J. Holmes,** *$22.00 – 25.00.*

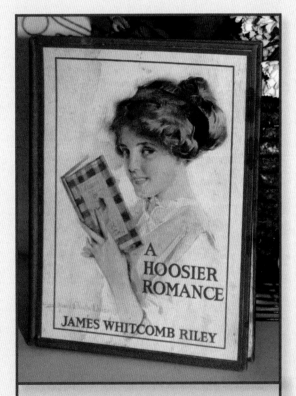

Antique romance novel, pretty cover, **Hoosier Romance, James Whitcomb Riley,** *$22.00 – 25.00.* Courtesy of Coffee Trade Antiques.

Book page, Harrison Fischer, pretty image, $10.00 – 15.00. Courtesy of www.vintagepastelle.com.

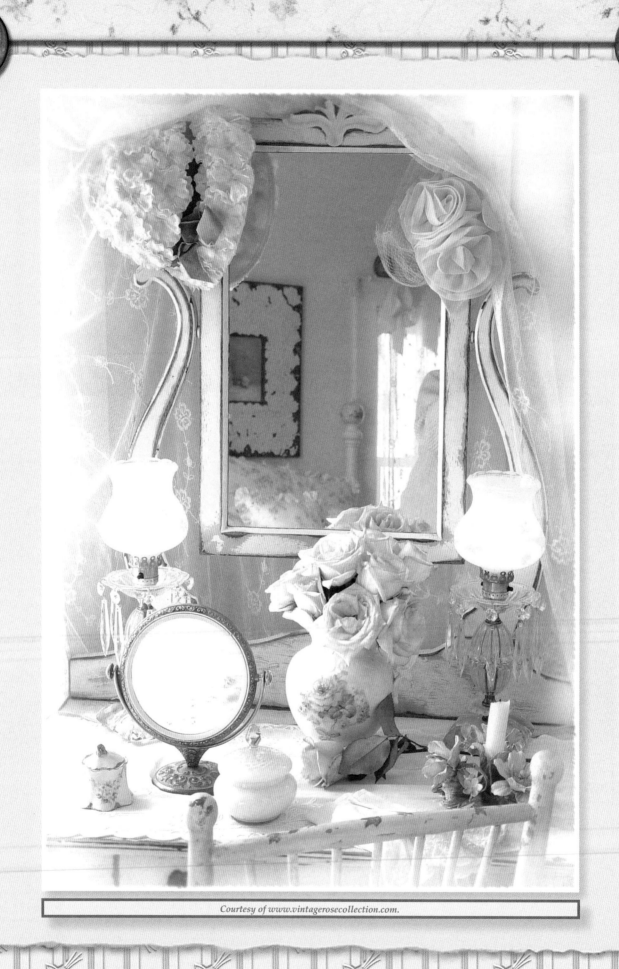

Courtesy of www.vintagerosecollection.com.

Vanity

Bone China Bouquets
Picture Frames
Powder Room
Rhinestone Clocks
Shabby Mirrors
Shabby Vanity
Vanity Furniture
Vanity Trays & Accessories
Vases
Wash Bowls

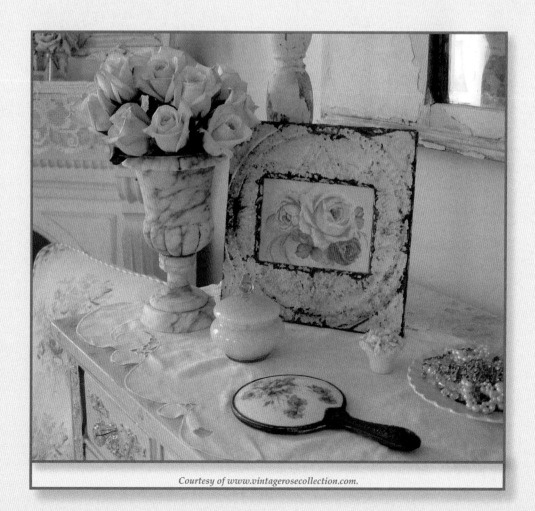

Courtesy of www.vintagerosecollection.com.

*I*f there is one place in a romantic cottage style home for pretty and pink it is the vanity area. Soft fabrics, florals, china roses, floral wall décor, antique white wicker, chippy painted shelves, pretty vanity vases, perfume bottles, vanity trays, and accessories are always popular collectibles.

Hat boxes are not only colorful accessories but great places for storage. Jewelry can be draped over mirrors or lamps. (See the chapter on How to Display, Store & Use Vintage Finds.)

Consider taking the doors off an old medicine cabinet and adding glass shelves for a delightful curio cabinet to display your perfumes, half dolls, and powder jars. Or collage an old cabinet with pretty vintage postcards (see the chapter Pretty in Print).

Bone China Bouquets

China bouquet, bone, Royale Stratford, $25.00 – 45.00. *Courtesy of www.ticklemepinkboutique.com.*

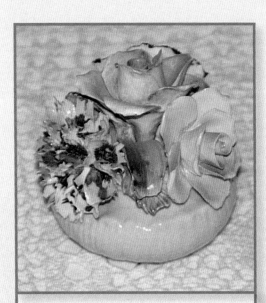

China bouquet, Radnor Bone China, England, $25.00 – 45.00. *Courtesy of www. ticklemepinkboutique.com.*

China bouquet, Radnor Bone China, England, $25.00 – 45.00. *Courtesy of www.ticklemepinkboutique.com.*

China bouquet, Royal Staffordshire, $25.00 – 145.00. *Courtesy of www.stacysshabbyshoppe.com.*

Picture Frames

Frame, celluloid, 1920s, $12.00 – 15.00. *Courtesy of Coffee Trade Antiques.*

Frame, metal, $15.00. *Courtesy of Coffee Trade Antiques.*

Frame, shabby cast iron, repainted, $35.00 – 55.00. *Courtesy of www. fadedrosecottage.com.*

Powder Room

Waste basket, metal, hand painted, 1930s, $65.00 – 75.00. *Courtesy of www.cottagerags.com.*

Waste basket, metal, hand painted, 1930s, $45.00 – 65.00. *Courtesy of www.cottagerags.com.*

Medicine cabinet, 1930s, wood, shabby style, collaged, hand painted, vintage perfume labels, $145.00-165.00. *Courtesy of www.vintagepastelle.com.*

Medicine cabinet, 1950s, oak, re-created with tin sign front, reclaimed frame with drop down door, $95.00 – 115.00. *Courtesy of www.vintagepastelle. com.*

Rhinestone Clocks

Vintage clock, made in France by Endura, faux pearls, beads, and rhinestones, $25.00 – 75.00. *Courtesy of www.inthepinkantiques.com.*

Vintage clock, made in Germany by Phinney-Walker, clear crystals/rhinestones, $25.00 – 65.00. Courtesy of www.inthepinkantiques.com.

Vintage clock, made in Germany by Phinney-Walker, pink crystals/rhinestones, $25.00 – 50.00. Courtesy of www.inthepinkantiques.com.

Vintage clock, made in Germany by Semca, pink crystals/rhinestones, $25.00 – 75.00. Courtesy of www.inthepinkantiques.com.

Pink and clear rhinestone vintage clock, made by Walker Phinney, circa 1950, $95.00. Courtesy of www.vintageprettyandpink.com.

Shabby Mirrors

Mirror (new base), vintage broken Limoges, Austrian, and Bavarian china, and Lefton china angel, handcrafted by artist Carey Chelenza of www.dishnchips. com, $375.00.

Mirror embellished with vintage china mosaic pieces, artist Penny Carlson of www.lavenderhillstudio.com, $220.00 − 250.00.

Vintage mirror, hand painted, $125.00 − 200.00. Courtesy of www. stacysshabbyshoppe.com.

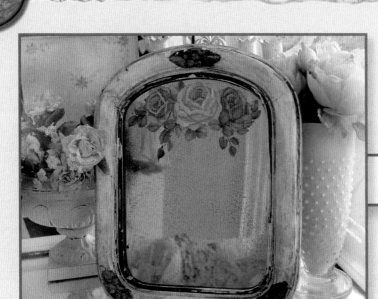

Vintage mirror, hand painted by artist Jo-Anne Colleti of www. vintagerosecollection.com, $125.00.

Shabby Vanity

Vintage wooden drawer from old sewing machine painted white, distressed, decorated with roses, lined with floral fabric, $39.00 – 45.00. Courtesy of www.soshabbypink.com.

Old wooden box lid, hand painted, distressed, and decorated with pink roses, $35.00 – 40.00. Courtesy of www. soshabbypink.com.

Old wooden jointed shoe form, painted pink and embellished with large pink rose, distressed, $25.00 – 30.00. *Courtesy of www.soshabbypink.com.*

Vintage electric radio, hand painted pink, decorated with acrylic door knob and roses, distressed, $40.00 – 45.00. *Courtesy of www.soshabbypink.com.*

Old, rusty wind-up clock, painted white and embellished with roses, distressed, $25.00 – 30.00. *Courtesy of www.soshabbypink.com.*

Vintage wooden drawer from old sewing machine, painted a soft cottage green, distressed, decorated with roses, lined with pink wallpaper, $39.00 – 45.00. *Courtesy of www.soshabbypink.com.*

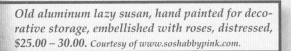

Old aluminum lazy susan, hand painted for decorative storage, embellished with roses, distressed, $25.00 – 30.00. *Courtesy of www.soshabbypink.com.*

Vanity mirror embellished with vintage china mosaic pieces, artist Penny Carlson of www.lavenderhillstudio. com, $400.00 – 450.00.

Tissue box, embellished with vintage china mosaics, artist Penny Carlson of www.lavenderhillstudio. com, $70.00 – 80.00.

Vanity Furniture

Vanity table with mirror, hardwood, painted, 1920s, $200.00 – 400.00. *Courtesy of www.bellarosadesigns.com.*

Vintage vanity and bench, painted white, original hardware, mid 1900s, $395.00 – 450.00. *Courtesy of www. bellarosecottage.com.*

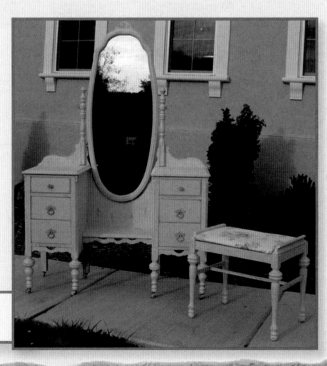

Vintage vanity with belle mirror and bench, painted pink, original hardware, 1930s, $400.00 – 500.00. *Courtesy of www.bellarosecottage.com.*

Victorian carved vanity, tri-fold mirror, early 1900s, $375.00 – 475.00. Courtesy of www.pinkpigwestport.com.

Vanity/desk, kidney shaped, painted white, original hardware, mid 1900s, $425.00 – 475.00. Courtesy of www.bellarosecottage.com.

Vanity, kidney shaped, painted, 1940s, $150.00 – 175.00. Courtesy of www.pinkpigwestport.com.

Vanity, original paint, 1930s, $125.00 – 150.00; vanity bench, mahogany, painted white, reupholstered, $50.00 – 75.00. *Courtesy of www.preservecottage.com.*

Bench, chippy painted, wood, newly recovered seat, $65.00 – 105.00. *Courtesy of www.fadedrosecottage.com.*

Vintage bench, mahogany, painted creamy white, accented with vintage china mosaics and stained glass, the top is covered in a vintage reproduction bark cloth, $125.00 – 175.00. *Courtesy of www.lavenderhillstudio.com.*

Victorian mirror, tin, $250.00 – 350.00. Courtesy of www.pinkpigwestport.com.

Vanity Trays & Accessories

Bath canister, glass, white and gold, 1900 – 1920s, $45.00 – 65.00. Courtesy of www.fadedrosecottage.com.

Trinket tray, gold heart, metal, $8.00 – 12.00. Courtesy of www.fadedrose.com.

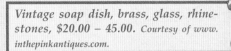

Vintage soap dish, brass, glass, rhinestones, $20.00 – 45.00. *Courtesy of www.inthepinkantiques.com.*

Vintage jewelry box, brass and rhinestones, $25.00 – 45.00. *Courtesy of www.inthepinkantiques.com.*

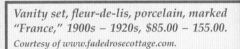

Vanity set, fleur-de-lis, porcelain, marked "France," 1900s – 1920s, $85.00 – 155.00. *Courtesy of www.fadedrosecottage.com.*

Vanity tray, porcelain, unmarked, $35.00 – 40.00. *Courtesy of www.preservecottage.com.*

Vanity set, 1930s, pink wicker tray, hand painted metal lids on glass jars, probably used in a nursery, $65.00 – 95.00. *Courtesy of www.vinatgepastelle.com.*

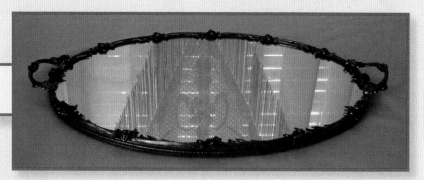

Dresser tray, vintage, gilded rose and leaf, 1950s, $55.00 – 65.00. *Courtesy of www. victoriasvintageshoppe.com.*

Powder jar, early 1900s, $50.00 – 65.00. *Courtesy of www.victoriasvintageshoppe. com.*

Hair receiver, Nippon, hand painted, $60.00 – 80.00. *Courtesy of www.victoriasvintageshoppe.com.*

Vases

Miniature floral urn vase, porcelain, $8.00 – 16.00. *Courtesy of www.fadedrosecottage. com.*

Ceramic pitcher/vase, unmarked, $65.00 – 75.00. *Courtesy of www.fadedrosecottage. com.*

Antique pitcher, porcelain, unmarked, 1800s, $75.00 – 225.00. *Courtesy of www. inthepinkantiques.com.*

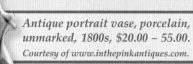

Antique portrait vase, porcelain, unmarked, 1800s, $20.00 – 55.00. *Courtesy of www.inthepinkantiques.com.*

Antique goddess vase, porcelain,
unmarked, 1800s, $45.00 – 95.00.
Courtesy of www.inthepinkantiques.com.

Vase, hand-painted bisque, $32.00.
Courtesy of Coffee Trade Antiques.

Vase, heart shaped, ceramic, $18.00 –
24.00. *Courtesy of Coffee Trade Antiques.*

Wash Bowls

Shaving mug, porcelain, unmarked, $35.00 – 65.00. Courtesy of www. inthepinkantiques.com.

Pitcher and bowl set, ceramic, $65.00 – 85.00. Courtesy of www.fadedrosecottage.com.

Pitcher and bowl set, enamelware, Portugal, $75.00 – 85.00. Courtesy of www.westportpinkpig.com.

Shaving mug, porcelain, Bavaria, ca. 1895 – 1935, $20.00 – 45.00. Courtesy of www.inthepinkantiques.com.

Antique pitcher and bowl set, broken handle, Mellor & Co., Etruia, flawless, $250.00, as shown $75.00. Courtesy of www.teacupsandtwigs.com.

Pitcher and bowl set, white, 1900s, $150.00 – 200.00. Courtesy of www.westportpinkpig.com.

Courtesy of Elizabeth Holcombe.

Sew Cottage-Y

Barkcloth & Drapery Pillows
Barkcloth Totes
Buttons
Dress Forms
Embroidered Pillows
Fabrics
Feedsack Pillows
Hanky Pillows & Accessories
Hanky Totes
Needlepoint Pillows
Vintage Sewing Projects
Vogart
Whimsical Pincushions

Courtesy of www.arosewithoutathorn.com.

This chapter is one of my favorites. I adore vintage textiles and fabrics and applaud the women who have the patience and talent to create fabulous usable works of art out of old drapes, embroidered towels, hankies, needlepoint, salvage, trim, and sewing notions. A little bit of creativity can go a long way. Millinery trim can be taken off old hats which are no longer in wearing condition. I have pulled feathers, flowers, buckles, and jeweled charms off hats and used them in many new ways. Photo contributor Elizabeth Holcombe likes to use vintage cotton fabric, millinery supplies, and older ceramic novelty figurines when she creates her darling pin cushions shown in this section. Single salt shakers combined with vintage tassels make great shade pulls.

Never throw out stained or damaged older tablecloths. Torn colorful 1940s –1950s tablecloths called "cutters" are often used to make delightful pillows, window shades, handbags, purses, aprons, or linings for glass closet doors, shelves, or room screens. Barkcloth salvage with vibrant botanicals or mid-century abstracts is highly collectible. Even barkcloth scraps are in demand as designers use them for trim on clothing, pocketbooks, or artwork.

When you come across old linens, doilies, lace, trim, hankies, dresser scarves, and other fabrics that look wimpy, yellowed, or have tears, give them a new life in a collage, as a background for framing, as part of a pillow, etc. Cottage is all about re-inventing what you have. I can't wait to show you all the fabulous sewing projects in this chapter. Get ready for a delightful chapter.

Barkcloth & Drapery Pillows

Barkcloth gets its name from a primitive fabric which is made from the fibers of tree bark found in tropical and subtropical countries. The outer bark is stripped from the tree and then the inner bark is separated from the outer bark. Next the inner bark is beaten with wooden beaters or steel tools on an anvil to spread the fibers. Often water and soaking may be introduced to soften the fibers. Larger cloths are made by layering and felting smaller pieces together during the beating phase. Sometimes a starchy glue-like substance derived from tropical plants is used to attach small pieces together. Primitive barkcloth was used for clothing and wall hangings.

Barkcloth made its way to France in the 1920s and was made using cotton mixed with rayon. Our introduction to barkcloth was the imported material from France known as cretonne, a woven cloth with a nubby texture. By the late 1930s barkcloth was being manufactured in America. During the colorful era (1940s – 1950s) barkcloth, a generic term to describe nubby fabric with a bark-like texture dominated American households. From upholstered furnishings to window treatments barkcloth was favored because of its durability and dense weave. I have heard people claim that barkcloth is so strong that it is cat proof. I'd love to hear from readers about this observation; I have my doubts.

Florals, country scenes, geometrics, abstracts, botanicals, landscapes, leaves, and birds are all common designs found on barkcloth. Today there are many design houses reproducing barkcloth using older designs. When buying barkcloth be sure to ask if what you are buying is vintage or new. Atomic era barkcloth with geometric and abstract designs by noted artists in large quantities is very hard to find. If you discover a website that shows so much inventory that you think you have gone to heaven and back...beware...you are probably looking at a reproduction studio. Most times, you will find a yard or two here and there. It's not common to hit the jackpot anymore with these vintage textiles. Expect to pay $10.00 – 25.00 a yard for vintage barkcloth.

Cushion made from vintage salvaged linen from curtains and vintage chenille, 1950s, $60.00. Courtesy of www. vintageprettyandpink.com.

Cushion made from vintage fabrics, French roses barkcloth, ticking, curtain fabrics from Paris flea markets, 1920s to 1950s. $60.00. *Courtesy of www. vintageprettyandpink.com.*

Barkcloth pillow, 1940s, Glencourt pattern barkcloth, remade pillow, 18", $85.00. *Courtesy of www.vintagepastelle.com.*

Vintage ticking and barkcloth pillow, 1930s, remade, 20", $115.00. *Courtesy of www.vintagepastelle.com.*

Barkcloth Totes

The totes shown in this section are from the textile studios of Elizabeth Holcombe (elizabethholcombe.com). Elizabeth plans her one of a kind bags around vibrant botanical vintage barkcloth and then coordinates complementary vintage embellishments, trim, and new materials. Her colorful totes sell for $42.00 – 45.00. That's a great price for so much handcrafted work!

Buttons

The buttons and sewing notions shown here are from the 1940s – 1950s and would sell for $2.00 – 5.00 a card. Often these gems can be found mixed in a lot contained in an old sewing basket or tin. With the refound interest in knitting and other home sewing, arts, vintage buttons are popular today. You will note that many cottage style collectors like to embellish their handmade pillows with pastel colored buttons and other trinkets which complement floral fabric quite well. Debra J. Wisniewski's book *Antique & Collectible Buttons* is a good resource for the button enthusiast. Photographs in this section are the courtesy of Primrose Design.

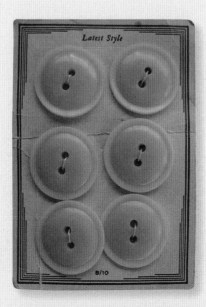

29¢ le chic
GUARANTEED WASHABLE

5866—22 (⅝")7on PINK   357

JAPAN

10¢

Guaranteed to Wash and Dry Clean

10¢

and Dry Clean

TRIMTEX

10¢

Rayon
RICK
RACK

FOR NEAT
TRIMMING OF
• DRESSES
• APRONS
• JACKETS
• SUITS

4 YARDS FAST COLOR No. 815

NOBLEM
GUARANTEED RUSTPROOF

SIZE: 2/0

MADE IN CZECHOSLOVAKIA

WASHABLE

Mannequin by A Rose Without A Thorn, dress form, vintage feedsack, lower front view, mid twentieth century, $425.00.

Dress Forms

There is nothing plain and simple in Maureen Reid's cottage style home in Florida. Maureen, owner of www.arosewithoutathorn.com is always busy taking vintage finds and creating beautiful decorative pieces. She has even found a way to dress up a dress form before the dress goes on it. Take a look at how she covers these mannequins with vintage feedsacks.

Yes, the adorned dress forms shown here are up there in price, but hours go into these works of art. Just for the record, you can usually pick up ordinary dress forms for about $45.00. Sometimes I will go months without seeing a dress form and at other times I keep bumping into them... literally!

Back view

Mannequin, handmade by A Rose Without A Thorn, dress form, vintage feedsack, lower front view, mid twentieth century, $425.00.

Front view

Embroidered Pillows

Pillow, Vogart, cotton, hand embroidered, early twentieth century, $45.00 – 55.00. Courtesy of www.arosewithoutathorn.com.

Pillow, linen, tinted, embroidered, 1940s, $35.00 – 45.00. Courtesy of www.cottagerags.com.

Pillow, embroidered, Vogart, 1930s, $30.00 – 40.00. *Courtesy of www.preservecottage.com.*

Pillow, handmade by Primrose Design, vintage appliquéd, towel, new cotton fabrics, and vintage buttons, new, $36.00.

Tote, one of a kind, made from vintage embroidered towel and embellished with new and vintage trim, textile artist Elizabeth Holcombe of www.elizabethholcombe.com, $42.00 – 45.00.

Fabrics

Janet of Primrose Design introduced me to a great online resource for the vintage textile collector and sewing crafter. You will find a goldmine of information and resources at www. fabrics.net. This is a wonderful group of gals who write columns and articles about textiles as well as serve as an active community for individuals who want to buy and sell textiles or read about their favorite fabrics and projects. In a recent visit to the site I came across these terrific articles as well as so many others for cottage style collectors: "A Guide to Slipcovers," "How to Clean & Maintain Upholstery," "Quilt Patterns," "Book Reviews," "Creating Lampshades," "Fabric Care," "Fabric Identification."

Fabric prices: Swatches shown here are cotton, polished cotton, and seasucker. Expect to pay $8.00 – 10.00 a yard. Feedsack is more, $15.00 – 20.00.

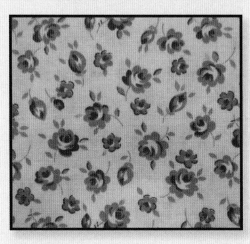

Feedsack Pillows

After the 1846 invention of the sewing machine, food products such as grain, seed, and animal feed were able to be stored and transported in bags rather than boxes and barrels. The original feedbags, also called feedsacks, were initially made of heavy canvas, and were used to obtain flour, sugar, meal, grain, salt, and feed from the mills. Feedbags remained popular from the late 1840s to the 1890s. They were reusable, with the farmer bringing an empty sack stamped with his mark or brand to the mill to be filled. Feedbags as they were known then, were initially printed on plain white cloth and in sizes that corresponded to barrel sizes.

After soaking the feedbags in lye or bleach to get rid of the labels, women who lived on farms would turn these feedsacks into usable items such as dish cloths, diapers, nightgowns, and other household items. Manufacturers decided to take advantage of this and started offering sacks in various prints and solid colors as a marketing tool to create loyalty. It would take three identical sacks to make a dress, for example, and the farmer just might be induced to buy more that way. In *Feed Sack Quilt History: Feedsacks, Frugal and Fun*, Judy Anne Johnson Breneman writes about a woman whose undergarments revealed the phrase "southern best." Magazines and pattern companies began to take notice of feedsack popularity and by the 1920s began to publish particular patterns to take advantage of the feedsack prints. According to Janet McCaffrey of www.primrosedesign.com, who contributed many of the photographs in this chapter, there is a popular urban myth claiming that 15,000 feedsack patterns have been printed over the years. At the height of feedsack production there were dozens of mills in operation continuing production of these fabrics through the 1960s. If you would like to see a lovely sampling of feedsack designs, take a look at The Feedsack Pattern Gallery on Janet's website www.primrosedesign.com.

Feedsacks were used eventually to make clothes, toys, underwear, aprons, pillowcases, diapers, laundry bags, curtains, table cloths, towels, and dish cloths. Some of the more collectible sacks now are those with Walt Disney themes such as Davy Crockett, Cinderella, and Alice in Wonderland; movie themes such as Gone With the Wind; comic book themes such as Buck Rogers; and nursery rhyme themes such as Little Bo Peep and Humpty Dumpty according to "The Wonderful World of Feedsack Fabric," EBAY Collector's Guides ("craftmule" October 22, 2007).

After WWII, technological innovations made the use of a feedbag less popular, as storage for the products traditionally kept in feedbags became cheaper in heavy plastic containers. Some Midwest, Amish, and Mennonite communities in the United States still use feedbags today.

Making practical items from feedsacks is not just limited to farmwives, today many young women with an interest in sewing are searching flea markets, grandma's attic, and online for feedsack fabric.

A delightful website, getcrafty.com, dubbed the "home of the craftistas" is a great resource for crafters and one of the sources for background information on this topic. See Kayte Terry, "Feedsacks, a Tradition of Recycling and Repurposing," September 13, 2007, www.getcrafty.com.

Pillow, A Rose Without A Thorn, cotton, vintage feedsack and crochet, mid twentieth century, $75.00.

Pillow, handmade by A Rose Without A Thorn, cotton, vintage feedsack and crochet, twentieth century, $75.00.

Pillow, handmade by A Rose Without A Thorn, cotton, vintage feedsack and crochet, mid twentieth century, $75.00.

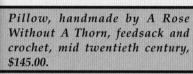

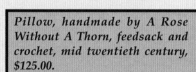

Pillow, handmade by A Rose Without A Thorn, feedsack and crochet, mid twentieth century, $145.00.

Pillow, handmade by A Rose Without A Thorn, feedsack and crochet, mid twentieth century, $125.00.

Pillow, handmade by A Rose Without A Thorn, feedsack, crochet and cotton, mid twentieth century, $75.00.

Pillow, handmade by A Rose
Without A Thorn, kitten feedsack,
crochet, ticking, and embroidered
linen, mid twentieth century,
$145.00.

Hanky Pillows & Accessories

Hankies once sat in grandma's dresser drawers. Now everyone has found a new use for these delicate accessories. You will note crafters who convert hankies into pillows, framed artwork, pocketbooks, shelf trim, doll covers, quilts, clothing embellishments, etc. Of particular interest to collectors who adore the romantic cottage style is hankies that have colorful floral patterns or scalloped edges. Whimsical hankies such as nursery rhymes, children's themes, holiday designs, and animals are also very popular among collectors. Although I have seen very unusual hankies fetch higher than average prices, for the most part, you can find an ample supply of these delightful items for $2.00 – 6.00. By the way, there is no need to buy wimpy, wrinkled, yellowed hankies because there are plenty of nicely pressed fresh vintage ones out there waiting for a new home.

Pillow, handmade by www.primrosedesign.
com, vintage handkerchiefs and buttons, re-
created new, $48.00.

Pillow, handmade by www.primrosedesign.
com, vintage handkerchiefs and buttons, re-
created new, $36.00.

Handkerchiefs, vintage cotton with crochet edging, $2.00 – 5.00 each.
Courtesy of www.primrosedesign.com.

Handmade by www.primrosedesign.com, sachet made from vintage handkerchiefs and buttons, re-created new, $16.00.

Hanky Totes

The totes shown in this section are from the textile studios of Elizabeth Holcombe (www.elizabethholcombe.com). Elizabeth plans her one-of-a-kind bags around vintage hankies and then coordinates complimentary vintage embellishments, trim, and new materials. Her colorful totes sell for $42.00 – 45.00. That's a great price for so much handcrafted work!

Needlepoint Pillows

The photographs in this section are examples of the fine handcrafted work of Sharon Wollman of www.cestchouettehome. com. Sharon's pillows are made from vintage needlepoint that are rescued from their past and redesigned using both vintage and new trim. As with other textile crafts shown in this chapter, designers are reclaiming the beauty of traditional home accessories and changing them to work well in contemporary cottage style homes, where old is new again.

Think about all the hours that went into making the needlepoint in the first place and then the additional hours Sharon spends re-assembling these textiles to create one-of- a-kind gorgeous pillows. Sharon has told me that the vintage needle-

point comes from old pillows, framed pieces, or needlepoint once destined to be a seat cover and never used. (See examples below.) While prices vary according to the age, rarity, and condition of these cherished treasures, you can easily find lots of raw materials (old needlepoint) priced inexpensively ($10.00 – 30.00) as well as higher end options.

After Sharon discovers an older piece at a flea market, tag sale, or collectible's shop, she returns home to her sewing studio and gets to work, coordinating silks, fabrics, trim, and embellishments to complement the palette and look of the older needlepoint. Sharon's pillows shown below are very fairly priced at $65.00. Be sure to take a look at her website at www.cestchouettehome.com for her latest works of art!

Vintage Sewing Projects

Half doll, porcelain, German, pin cushion, early twentieth century. This sweet half doll pincushion has been made with a mixture of vintage trims, rhinestones, and new fabrics. The base of the half doll includes wonderful French lavender buds for a lovely fragrance and stands 9" tall, $35.00 – 50.00. Courtesy of www.arosewithoutathorn.com.

Bag, handmade by A Rose Without A Thorn, cotton, vintage crochet, damask, and fabric, 1940s, $75.00 – 100.00.

The Tussie Mussie

I asked Maureen Reid, owner of www.arosewithoutathorn.com and the gifted textile crafter who made The Tussie Mussies below, to discuss the custom of giving a Tussie Mussie. She offers this explanation: "The Tussie Mussie is thought to have originated from France, but it was during the Victorian era in England that it reached its full popularity. The Tussie Mussie have long been known as the 'talking bouquet.' This is a very appropriate name for the little poesy or nosegay of flowers because of the hidden message they were able to convey.

A suitor would spend considerable time carefully selecting his flowers of choice, with the central flower composed of a beautiful rose. During the Victorian era many flowers were given a specific meaning and this translated into a hidden message in the bouquet, hence the term 'talking bouquet.' The young lady that received this poesy would take the time to look up the meaning of the flowers that were included in the nosegay. There were many books produced that would help both the suitor and the recipient read the message that was in the bouquet.

These make a wonderful tradition for a bride or a loved one today and can still bring a smile to a special person's face.

What could be a lovelier 'new' tradition to begin today, if you simply want to say thank you or you are loved, there is nothing like giving a Tussie Mussie."

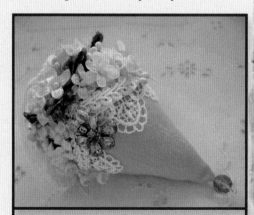

Tussie Mussie, European origin, vintage millinery flowers, silk and antique crystals, French lavender filling, $35.00. Courtesy of www.arosewithoutathorn.com.

Tussie Mussie, European origin, vintage millinery flowers and rhinestones, French lavender filling, $35.00. Courtesy of www.arosewithoutathorn.com.

Vogart

The Vogart pillow cases shown here are courtesy of www. preservecottage.com. These examples sell for $25.00 – 30.00.

Whimsical Pincushions

The charming handcrafted pincushions shown in this section were created as one-of-a-kind whimsical sewing acces-sories by Elizabeth Holcombe of www.elizabethholcombe.com. Her attractive pincushions are made from vintage ornaments, millinery trim, embellishments, and a combination of vintage and new fabric and sell for $22.00 – 26.00.

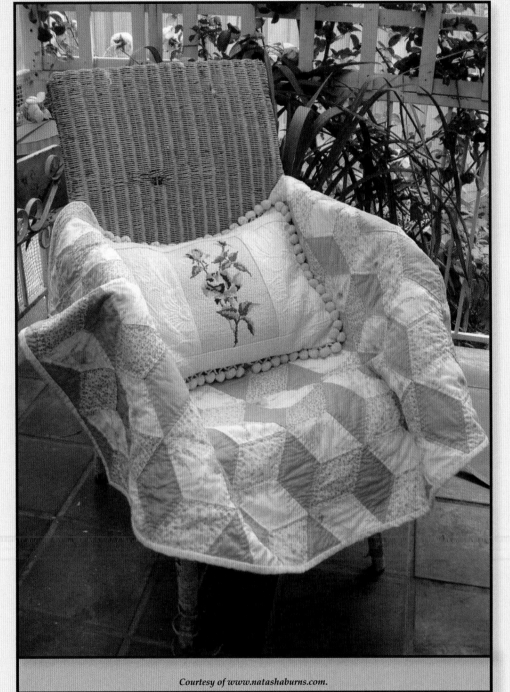

Courtesy of www.natashaburns.com.

On the Porch

Birdcages
Sofa, Benches & Seating
Wicker Chairs
Wicker & Wood Tables

Courtesy of www.vintagepastelle.com.

Front porches are very cottage-y. What a better way to relax than sitting on your porch and enjoying your colorful cottage garden, seascape, or mountain view. Porches can be viewed as rooms according to popular designer Kitty Bartholomew. She advises thinking about your porch as having walls, a ceiling, and a floor even if you have to create these features by using architectural salvage or vintage finds to accomplish your goal. For example, you can create an interesting back drop (wall support) with a vintage garden trellis or old door panel. From these newly created walls you can then hang plants, decorative plates, old garden tools, etc. Porch floors can be painted, stained, and accessorized with synthetic rugs. Choosing a color palette and style outdoors is just as important as the attention given to inside room interiors. Whether you are after a "beachy" look, romantic style, or a rustic feeling, there are many furnishings, textiles, and collectibles shown throughout this book which can also be used outside. Kitty Bartholomew loves to bring inside what is often used outside and the other way around as well, adorning porches with objects you never thought of using. Let the creativity begin! (Bartholomew, Kitty 2005.)

In this chapter you will see photographs of porch favorites such as wicker, birdcages, and benches. You will also find many porch collectibles in the next chapter, Cottage Garden.

Birdcages

While working on this book, I fell in love with birdcages. Although I had really never paid attention to them before I was now on the hunt for cages and learned to look up when I went shopping in antique malls and quaint shops. But of course many gorgeous elaborate cages stand tall or are displayed as table top pieces. The more common mass produced cages from the colorful eras (1920s, 1930s, 1940s) have climbed in price and are snapped up easily. Once a $30.00 – 45.00 dollar item, they are now selling for twice as much in many areas. Recently I found a funky, newer, very large, handmade, whimsical cage that was sitting on the porch of an antique shop in a beach town. I suppose because it was 10 degrees out, the owner of this shop was eager to part with this piece. He had a price of $25.00 on the cage and I can't believe I left without it. In fact I'm going to call him in the morning to see if it's still without a home. I did forget to tell you it was painted lime green... but I liked it!

Early architectural cages of the nineteenth century can go for thousands of dollars. Whether you adore rustic cages, classics, or the architectural variety, expect to see the full range of prices listed for these hot cottage collectibles. Look to auction houses and off-the-beaten-track little shops... you never know where a special birdcage may show up.

Early French and Dutch birdcages were brass and iron wire cages and associated with aristocrats. Early English cages were made of brass and mahogany.

During the Victorian era, birdcages were no longer simply for the very wealthy. Mass-produced ornate and attractive birdcages were easily found in Victorian parlors. There are many very well made reproductions out there so be careful when sinking money into what you believe is an antique birdcage (Garisto, Leslie, 1992).

Birdcage, sewing machine base, $120.00 – 150.00. Courtesy of www.preservecottage.com.

Birdcage, metal, 1930s – 1940s, $25.00 – 30.00. Courtesy of www.preservecottage.com.

Birdcage, vintage, wood and tin, 1930s, $75.00 – 95.00. *Courtesy of www.pinkpigwestport.com.*

Birdcage, cottage, iron, 1930s, $85.00 – 95.00. *Courtesy of www.pinkpigwestport. com.*

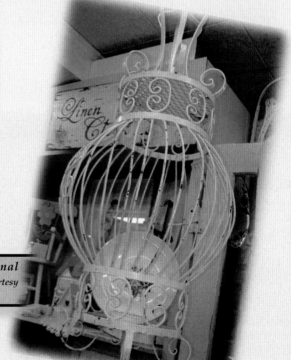

Bird cage, wrought iron, 1940s, original white paint with rust, $75.00 – 95.00. *Courtesy of www.romanticroseboutique.com.*

Sofa, Benches & Seating

Sofa, wicker, painted, reupholstered, 1920s, $400.00 – 600.00. Courtesy of www.preservecottage.com.

Wicker settee, Lloyd Loom Wicker, 1920s, $500.00 – 600.00. Courtesy of www.pinkpigwestport.com.

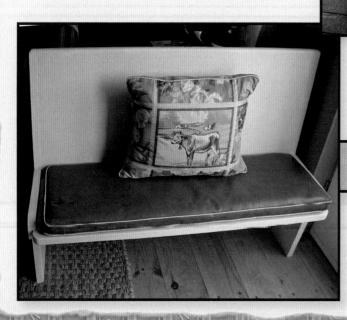

Bench, farmhouse type, 1930s, $150.00 – 250.00. Courtesy of www.pinkpigwestport.com.

Original Westport, NY, Railroad bench, 1900s, $600.00 – 800.00. *Courtesy of www.pinkpigwestport.com.*

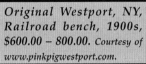

Vintage headboard bench, wood, remade bed into a bench, repainted, 1950s, $225.00 – 350.00. Courtesy of www.vintagepastelle.com.

Bench, farmhouse type, oak, $300.00 – 400.00. Courtesy of *www.pinkpigwestport.com.*

Wicker settee, Victorian high back, 1800s, $400.00 – 500.00. Courtesy of www.pinkpigwestport.com.

Wicker Chairs

Wicker has always been a favorite on porches. Popular during the Victorian era, the word wicker is actually derived from the Scandinavian words wika, meaning "bend" and vikker, meaning "willow." Although many people refer to "wicker" as a material, it is actually a catch all term to apply to many different materials which are woven.

Materials available for weaving depend on the climate of a given region. For example in warmer areas you will see reeds, palm leaves, canes, grasses, and, of course, rattan made into furniture. Crafters in cooler climates avail themselves to wood strips, rushes, wild grasses, willow twigs, and roots for designing furniture. Most of us are familiar with rattan, the most popular natural material for weaving. Because rattan is a solid core vine it is very sturdy and a good choice for furniture (Whitesides, Mary, 2003).

Wicker can be divided into several styles; Victorian, Art Deco, Bar Harbor, and stick wicker (modern). In this section you will see several different styles shown.

Wicker chair, Lusty Loom, 1920s, $175.00 – 275.00. Courtesy of www. pinkpigwestport.com.

Wicker chair, Lloyd Loom Wicker, 1930s, $100.00 – 150.00. Courtesy of www.pinkpigwestport.com.

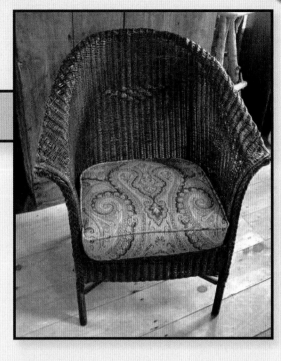

Wicker chair, Lloyd Loom, 1920s, $150.00 – 250.00. Courtesy of www. pinkpigwestport.com.

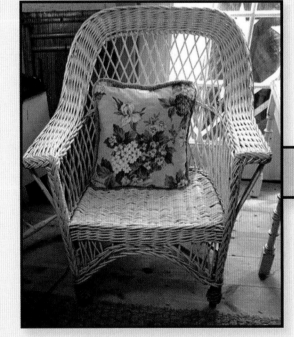

Wicker chair, Bar Harbour reed, 1930s, $200.00 – 250.00. Courtesy of www.pinkpigwestport.com.

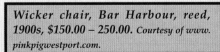

Wicker chair, Bar Harbour, reed, 1900s, $150.00 – 250.00. Courtesy of www. pinkpigwestport.com.

Chair, wicker, old paint, 1910s, $95.00 – 120.00. *Courtesy of www. preservecottage.com.*

Child's rocking chair, painted, 1920s, $85.00 – 100.00. *Courtesy of www.preservecottage.com.*

Wicker & Wood Tables

Cottage table, rattan and bamboo, 1940s, $125.00 – 130.00. *Courtesy of www.pinkpigwestport. com.*

Table, leather top, wicker, early 1900s, $150.00 – 200.00. *Courtesy of www.pinkpigwestport. com.*

Side table, Victorian, wicker, 1900s, $110.00 – 125.00. Courtesy of www.pinkpigwestport.com.

Victorian plant stand, 1900s, $75.00 – 100.00. Courtesy of www. pinkpigwestport.com.

Table, rustic, painted, reed and wood, 1940s, $250.00 – 350.00. Courtesy of www. pinkpigwestport.com.

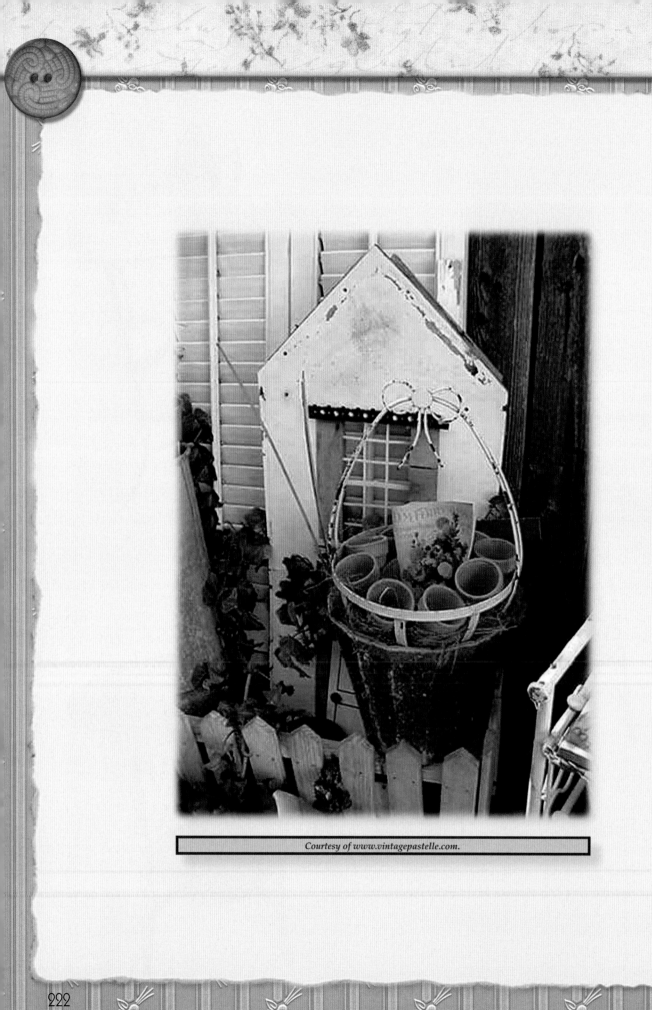

Courtesy of www.vintagepastelle.com.

Cottage Garden

Around the Garden
Benches
Bird Houses, Baths & Feeders
Garden Furniture
Garden Ornaments: Cement & Stone
Garden Ornaments: Wood
Garden Signs
Plant Stands & Holders
Planters & Flower Boxes
Sap Buckets: Hand Painted
Watering Cans

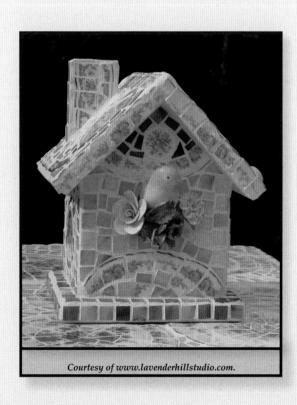

Courtesy of www.lavenderhillstudio.com.

ottage gardens associated with the English country-side are known for their colorful, informal, relaxed landscape and surroundings.

Today many cottage style collectors are after a more folksy look and hunt for garden collectibles and accessories which are charming, practical, and perhaps, a bit quirky. Found objects which are rusty, flaky, crackled, worn, chipped, and weathered are preferred over newer manufactured items.

Once you start playing with ideas, it is actually quite easy to find a great many of objects that can be used as planters, flower boxes, and outdoor decorative items. For example, old kettles, wood soda crates, old wash tubs, and oversized ceramic bowls are all wonderful basins or containers for plants and flowers.

Because cottage style is all about recycling and repurposing, what you have around your kitchen and in your storage areas for "orphaned" kitchen and housewares can be put to use in your sunroom, on your deck or patio. An enamelware coffee pot that has lost its top looks adorable with a hanging plant. Pyrex casseroles make sweet bases for "dish garden."

As I mentioned in the chapter titled How to Display, Store & Use Vintage Finds shelves and displays can be made from so many common older objects. During a recent visit to The Blue Willow antique shop in Granby Connecticut, Laura, the owner, showed me how she used a 1950s child's patio chair to serve as a neat "shelf" for potted plants. In another area of her shop she mounted vintage metal plant holders on an old white column which came off a friend's porch.

Despite the fact that it was frigid outside, Laura's shop was "blooming" with silk red geraniums sitting everywhere. I spotted geraniums sitting inside a 1940s handmade green flower box with red trim, on top of a yellow painted step ladder, on the seat of a chippy turquoise tot's chair, and inside a wooden garden tote.

All of these adorable garden items caught my eye because the colors of the shelves or containers were strong and matched well with the flowers. Reds (geraniums) go well with green, turquoise, yellow, etc. By the way, I came home with the whole kit and caboodle!

You already know from my first book, *Hot Kitchen & Home Collectibles of the 30s, 40s, 50s*, that I adore red and yellow! These colors are warm and bring me right back to grandma's porch in the 1950s with her red metal chairs and colorful rose bushes everywhere.

In contrast to bold colors, many romantic cottage collectors prefer whites and pastels in and around their gardens. Pam Daly of www.vintagepastelle.com sticks to pink, aqua, and soft green for her handmade vintage picket fence benches shown in this chapter. These cottage colors are also often seen in beach communities where a lighter look is fashionable.

Whether your tastes are for primary colors, pastels, or patriotic red, white and blue, you can have a lot of fun in and around your garden.

In this section you will find a good representation of popular cottage garden collectibles including garden tools, birdhouses, folk art, furniture, watering cans, garden signs, planters, and ornaments. Many of these items can easily be found at tag sales, flea markets, and second hand shops.

When you visit a tag sale and you do not see garden collectibles for sale, don't be afraid to inquire if the owner has some goodies hiding in their garage or tool shed that they are willing to part with. Many homeowners aren't aware that there is actually interest in old rusty hand tools, older terra cotta pots, vintage hand tools, flaky picket fences, etc. Pick neighborhoods with very old homes when you are out and about "junking" for garden tools and collectibles. My motto here is that "Thar's Gold in Them Thar Garden Sheds" .... well maybe not gold, but a lot of groovy, aged rusty garden and outdoor treasures.

Reproductions:

Reproduction vintage style garden accessories are plentiful. These objects are made so well, it's really easy to get fooled. Shop around, ask questions, learn which items are commonly reproduced such as sap buckets, gates, statues, etc. You can learn a great deal from shops that carry both new and vintage garden accessories by asking the owner or staff to show you some differences between new and old objects. While often a lower price marked on an item that generally yields more is a clue to a seasoned shopper that what they are looking at may not be an original. This is only a starting point. The beginner generally doesn't know what prices to expect which is why a review of the collectibles shown in this section is a helpful beginning. And you may get lucky, you may find some bargains that are priced reasonably and are in fact the real deal.

Around the Garden

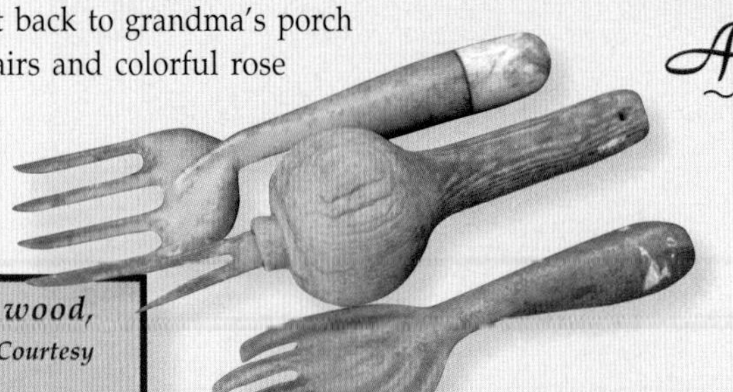

Garden tools, metal and wood, 1940s, $8.00 – 12.00 each. Courtesy of www.cottagerags.com.

Vintage garden rake, $25.00 – 45.00. *Courtesy of Country Cottage Florist.*

Oil can, metal, 1940s, $24.00 – 28.00. *Courtesy of www.cottagerags.com.*

Gas can, metal, painted, 1940s, $25.00 – 30.00. *Courtesy of www.cottagerags.com.*

Farm wheel barrel, primitive, 1900s, $100.00 – 200.00. *Courtesy of www.pinkpigwestport.com.*

Gocart, child's, hand-made, 1930s, $95.00 – 110.00. *Courtesy of www. pinkpigwestport.com.*

Vintage garden tote, hand painted in acrylics with pink roses and violet wild flowers, artist Susan Davenport of www. shabbycottagedesigns.com, $60.00.

Benches

Picket fence bench large, 1930s, wood, original creation, hand painted, $195.00. *Courtesy of www. vintagepastelle.com.*

Picket fence bench, 1930 – 1950s, wood, original design, repainted rose appliqués, $245.00. *Courtesy of www.vintagepastelle.com.*

Cottage bench, 1930s, wood, original paint, $135.00. Courtesy of www.vintagepastelle.com.

White picket fence hall tree bench, 1930s, wood, repainted, rose appliqués, Depression glass knobs, $235.00. Courtesy of www.vintagepastelle.com.

Bird Houses, Baths & Feeders

Purple martin house, wood, 1940s, $50.00 – 75.00. Courtesy of www.preservecottage.com.

Birdhouse, tin, primitive, 1940s, $75.00 – 85.00. Courtesy of www.pinkpigwestport.com.

Vintage, rustic and primitive hand-made bird house, painted cottage pastel colors, adorned with pink roses and distressed, $30.00 – 35.00. *Courtesy of www.soshabbypink.com.*

Vintage birdhouse, handcrafted, mosaic top of vintage English bone china, $150.00. *Courtesy of www. vintageprettyandpink.com.*

Birdhouse, double cottage, hand-made with antique ceiling tin and old barn wood, $45.00. *Courtesy of the www.vintagenest.com.*

Birdhouse, pink, on post, made with old barn wood, antique ceiling tin, old plaster cherub and antique prisms, $45.00. Courtesy of www.thevintagenest.com.

Birdhouse, wooden, painted pink and white, mounted on vintage porch post, accented with vintage ceiling tin and architectural items, $35.00 – 55.00. Courtesy of www.ticklemepinkboutique.com.

Bird house, handmade, vintage gold trim, $45.00. Courtesy of Coffee Trade Antiques.

Birdhouse embellished with vintage china mosaic pieces, artist Penny Carlson of www.lavenderhillstudio. com, $150.00 – 185.00

Wooden birdhouse embellished with vintage china mosaic pieces, artist, Penny Carlson of www.lavenderhillstudio.com, $150.00 – 185.00.

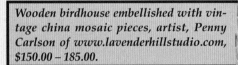

Birdbath created from a new iron birdbath and decorated with vintage china from 1800s to 1940s, artist Carey Chelenza of www. dishnchips.com, $200.00.

Garden Furniture

Bench, whimsical, birch, Adirondack style, 1940s, $140.00 – 160.00. Courtesy of www.pinkpigwestport.com.

Adirondack chair, original Westport chair, 1923, $1,500.00 – 1,800.00. Courtesy of www. pinkpigwestport.com.

Bench, whimsical, birch, Adirondack style, 1940s, $140.00 – 160.00. Courtesy of www.pinkpigwestport.com.

Primitive, wooden slat bench, 1900s, $100.00 – 200.00. *Courtesy of www. pinkpigwestport.com.*

Adirondack Westport chair, cedar, $500.00 – 600.00. Courtesy of www.pinkpigwestport.com.

Ferry seat, wood, $15.00 – 25.00. Courtesy of www.preservcottage.com.

Garden Ornaments:
Cement & Stone

Squirrel, cement, painted, 1940s, $20.00 – 25.00. *Courtesy of www.cottagerags.com.*

Duck, cement, 1940s, $15.00 – 20.00. *Courtesy of www.cottagerags.com.*

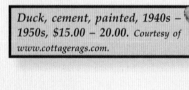

Duck, cement, painted, 1940s – 1950s, $15.00 – 20.00. *Courtesy of www.cottagerags.com.*

Boy and girl statue, cement, 1940s – 1950s, $150.00 – 175.00. *Courtesy of www.cottagerags.com.*

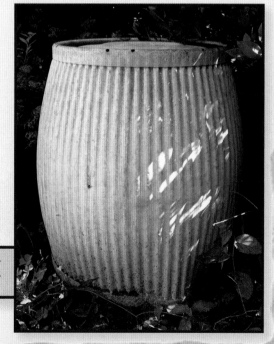

Dolly washer tub, galvanized metal, England, 1920s – 1930s, $50.00 – 75.00. *Courtesy of www.preservecottage.com.*

Chimney pot, Victorian, England, $90.00 – 125.00. Courtesy of www.preservecottage.com.

Chimney pot, Victorian, England, $90.00 – 125.00. Courtesy of www.preservecottage.com.

Duck, cement, 1940s, $50.00 – 60.00. Courtesy of www.pinkpigwestport. com.

Garden Ornaments: Wood

Doll bed planter, wood, original paint, 1940s, $75.00. *Courtesy of www.vintagepastelle. com.*

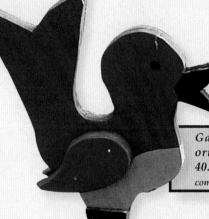

Garden ornament, bird, wood, original paint, 1930s, $35.00 – 40.00. *Courtesy of www.vintagepastelle. com.*

Garden ornament, girl, wood, original paint, as found, 1950s, $25.00 – 30.00. *Courtesy of www.vintagepastelle.com.*

Planter, bow, collage, 1930 – 1940s, metal, wood, papier mache, original paint, $115.00 – 135.00. *Courtesy of www.vintagepastelle.com.*

Garden ornament, wood, original paint, 1930s, $45.00 – 65.00. *Courtesy of www.vintagepastelle.com.*

Vintage Dutch girl windmill, wood, original paint, as found, 1940s, $48.00 – 60.00. *Courtesy of www.vintagepastelle.com.*

Garden Signs

Sign, vintage salvaged wood door, early 1900s, with beautiful shabby patina with original old chippy cream and sage green paint, newly hand-painted pink cottage roses and greenery, original hand-forged hardware, artist Susan Davenport of www.shabbycottagedesigns.com, $195.00.

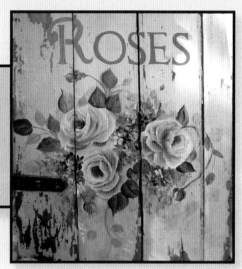

Sign, hand-painted roses, salvaged from a vintage headboard, 1930s, artist Susan Davenport of www.shabbycottagedesigns.com, $175.00.

Sign, antique window salvaged from an Italianate Victorian in Marietta, Ohio, artist Ronda Juniper Ray, $450.00.

Plant Stands & Holders

African violet plant stand, metal, 1950s, $45.00 – 50.00. *Courtesy of www.cottagerags.com.*

Plant stands, painted white, $25.00 each. *Courtesy of www.teacupsandtwigs.com.*

Bow metal planter, 1930s, original paint, $25.00 – 35.00. *Courtesy of www.vintagepastelle.com.*

Planters & Flower Boxes

Copper boiling pot, $120.00. *Courtesy of www.natashaburns.com.*

Half wine barrel, 1960s – 1970s, $90.00. Courtesy of www.natashaburns.com.

Full wine barrel, 1960s – 1970s, $120.00 – 150.00. Courtesy of www. natashaburns.com.

Cast iron planter, white, 1960s, $25.00 – 35.00. Courtesy of www. natashaburns.com.

French tin garden pails, 1900s, $55.00 – 75.00 for the three shown. *Courtesy of www. pinkpigwestport.com.*

Sap buckets, vintage, $25.00 each. *Courtesy of The Bleu Willow.*

Planter box, handcrafted, 1940s, $25.00 – 38.00. *Courtesy of The Bleu Willow.*

Vint tool tote, $75.00. *Courtesy of The Bleu Willow.*

Metal plant holder, $18.00; shears, rusted, $24.00. *Courtesy of The Bleu Willow.*

Flower pot chair, oak, painted, $15.00 – 25.00. *Courtesy of www.preservecottage.com.*

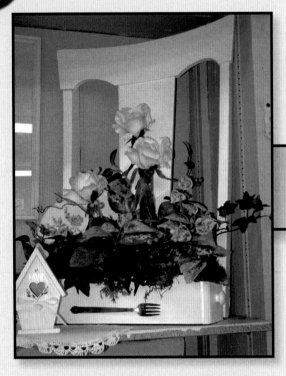

Chair back planter, early 1900s, oak chair back combined with new wooden box, repainted white, $50.00 – 75.00. Courtesy of www.romanticroseboutique.com.

Flower box, painted white, $25.00. Courtesy of www.teacupsandtwigs.com.

Ceramic crocks, unmarked, $55.00 – 65.00 each. Courtesy of www.fadedrosecottage.com.

Sap Buckets: Hand Painted

Bucket, galvanized tin, hand-painted sap container, mid twentieth century, $50.00 – 75.00. Courtesy of www.arosewithoutathorn.com.

Bucket, galvanized tin, hand-painted sap container, middle twentieth century, $50.00 – 75.00. Courtesy of www.arosewithoutathorn. com

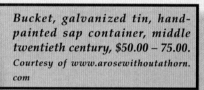

Bucket, galvanized tin, hand-painted sap container, middle twentieth century, $50.00 – 75.00. Courtesy of www.arosewithoutathorn. com.

Watering Cans

Watering cans can be found from different countries and in numerous shapes and patinas. Often a buyer confuses watering cans with early filling station cans used for engine fluids or hot-water cans used before the days of modern plumbing when the homeowner needed to fill wash basins. Hot water cans have lids to keep the water hot. All kinds of cans however have interest to collectors. Most watering cans I seem to come across are of the twentieth century houseplant variety either painted a color or left in a gray metal finish. The very early watering "cans" were earthenware pots. Watering cans can be found in copper and brass, tin plated, zinc-coated iron, and galvanized metal, representing different manufacturing stages in the evolution of this garden and houseplant collectible. During the Victorian era, attractive cans with long spouts prevailed. As plastics dominated the market in the late 1940s and 1950s, the metal took "second fiddle." Values depend on the age and design of a particular watering can. The common mid-century galvanized version can be found for $20.00 – 30.00. With advertising or a nice paint coat, add a few more dollars. Harder to find earlier watering

cans, European versions and Victorian era styles can sell for a great deal more money. Some people collect the full range of "cans" out there while other collectors narrow in their choices, hunting for only child-sized watering cans, or gooseneck spout types, lithographed ones, European types, early tole ones, painted varieties, etc.

The parts to the can are important to know about. The sprinkler head is called the "rose." It is very common to find this part missing from the can. Finding an intact can yields a premium price on older period pieces.

When the warmer weather returns you will see many antique dealers pulling out their garden items from storage and displaying these items. While it is easier to find watering cans during the spring and summer, you can generally get a better deal on your purchase if you find one sitting on a shelf in a shop the middle of the winter.

Cottage collectors love the worn look of vintage watering cans and are not upset to find rust, dings, peeling paint, scratches, etc. These imperfections are all part of the charm of these popular garden collectibles.

Watering can, metal, 1950s, $20.00 – 25.00. Courtesy of www.cottagerags.com.

Vintage galvanized watering cans, various sizes, $25.00 – 75.00 each. Courtesy of www.lavenderhillstudio.com.

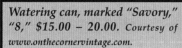

*Watering can, marked "Savory,"
"8," $15.00 – 20.00. Courtesy of
www.onthecornervintage.com.*

*Watering can, galvanized metal,
Germany, $30.00 – 35.00. Courtesy of www.
preservecottage.com.*

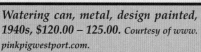

*Watering can, metal, design painted,
1940s, $120.00 – 125.00. Courtesy of www.
pinkpigwestport.com.*

Courtesy of www.pinkpigwestport.com.

At the Beach

Beachy Bath
Kitsch'N
On Deck
Red, White & Blue
Sail Away
Seaside Views

Courtesy of www.artfulcreations.biz.

*I*f you walk around your house hearing Jimmy Buffet tunes playing in your head then this type of cottage style is probably for you. While you need not live in Margaritaville to own a beach style cottage, you might consider packing away your dark heavy décor and furnishings. Coastal style is all about the colors of the tranquil ocean and surrounding seascape. Palettes of soft yellows, greens, pinks, and blues as well as white, ivory, peach, and aqua are very "beachy." If pastels are not for you, try "doing beach" with nautical colors such as, navy blue, red, and white.

Many of the collectibles associated with the 1950s were manufactured in "cottage colors" or patterned with tropical prints and beach novelty images. There are plenty of kitchen, bath, and bedroom accessories of this time period which go well with laid back beach cottages.

Chris Lankford, an obsessed collector of retro who has shared photographs of some of his collection in this section, advises collectors to become familiar with manufacturers who specialized in kitchenwares of the colorful era. They include Fire King, Gay Fad, Lincoln Beautyware, Blisscraft of Hollywood, Burroughs and Dapol Plastics, Federal Glass, and Lustro Ware. It's easy to find plenty of retro pastel colored plastic kitchenware, Pyrex, planters, and pottery.

For more about kitchenwares and collectibles be sure to take a look at my first book, *Hot Kitchen & Home Collectibles of the 30s, 40s, 50s* (Collectorbooks.com).

Not only can you accessorize your beach cottage kitchen with retro collectibles, but there are many other forties and fifties favorites that look terrific seaside. Barkcloth pillows and draperies, chenille bedspreads, white or pastel painted furniture, and wicker are great options.

Other beach cottage treasures are vintage anchors, life preservers, boats, lighthouses, lanterns, mermaids, fish, flamingos, and of course, seashell art and décor. Beachcombers love to look for sea glass, shells, dried sponges, pretty rocks, driftwood, and other found objects. Old glass candy and apothecary jars make wonder containers for your beach collections.

Many people enjoy using vintage salvage in their beach cottages. Lobster crates, old shutters, painted windows, barrels, fishing collectibles, weathered shelving or signs, and other flea market finds work great. Chippy painted furniture, cottage table and chairs, and charming cupboards and cabinets are all cottage favoroites.

Another direction to take when collecting for your seaside cottage is what some call cottage kitsch. This is still retro but with a bit more moxie. Think fun, colorful, whimsical. Collections of paint by number paintings, funky painted vintage tables, gravel art wall décor from the fifties, checkerboard floors, themed collections, mosaic accessories and furniture made from vintage broken plates and pottery, colorful fabrics with geometric or patterned designs, 1950s tablecloths and drapes with bold botanicals or travel themes are just the beginning. Here the art of mixing and matching pays off. Granny square afghans, folk art, and other handcrafted accessories may be just the right touch for a cottage home with some attitude!

Beachy Bath

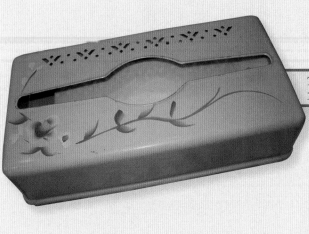

Tissue box, metal, Ransburg, $12.00 – 16.00. Courtesy of www.preservecottage.com.

Tissue box, metal, hand painted, 1940s, $22.00 – 26.00. Courtesy of www.cottagerags.com.

Hamper, metal, floral, pink, $25.00 – 45.00. Courtesy of Chris Lankford.

Planter, seafoam green, unmarked, $14.00. Courtesy of Coffee Trade Antiques.

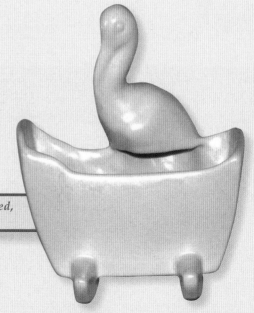

Planter, white pelican, unmarked, $16.00. Courtesy of Coffee Trade Antiques.

Planter, pink seashell, $18.00 – 18.00.
Courtesy of Coffee Trade Antiques.

Novelty Wallpaper

All the samples of bathroom novelty wallpaper are from www.Hannahstreasures.com, a vintage wallpaper specialty company. When ordering from Hannah's Treasures, expect to pay about $95.00 – 110.00 a roll with prices rising as the demand for these products are increasing.

Kitsch' N

Condiment set, pink, yellow, turquoise, with spoon and holders, $18.00 – 20.00. *Courtesy of Chris Lankford.*

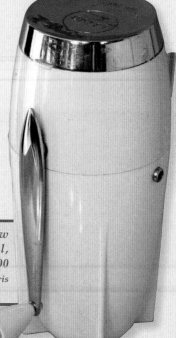

Ice crusher, yellow plastic and metal, rocket shaped, $12.00 – 15.00. *Courtesy of Chris Lankford.*

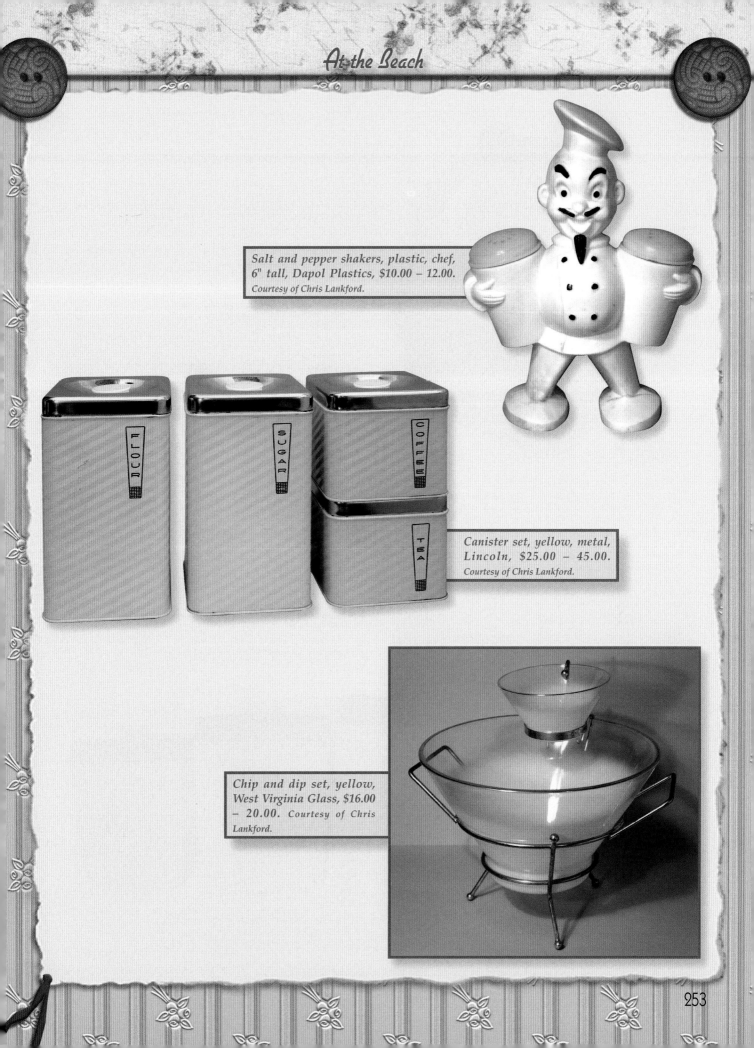

Salt and pepper shakers, plastic, chef, 6" tall, Dapol Plastics, $10.00 – 12.00. Courtesy of Chris Lankford.

Canister set, yellow, metal, Lincoln, $25.00 – 45.00. Courtesy of Chris Lankford.

Chip and dip set, yellow, West Virginia Glass, $16.00 – 20.00. Courtesy of Chris Lankford.

Pitcher, yellow and turquoise, plastic, $18.00 – 25.00. *Courtesy of Chris Lankford.*

Electric beater, Sunbeam, turquoise, $15.00 – 24.00. *Courtesy of Chris Lankford.*

FLOUR

SUGAR

COFFEE

TEA

Canister set, 1950s, pink, plastic, $25.00 – 30.00. *Courtesy of www.preservecottage.com.*

Restaurant quality dishes, assorted plates, $3.00 – 6.00 each. *Courtesy of www.preservecottage.com.*

Beverage glass, Arizona, Hazel Atlas, 1950s, $6.00 – 8.00 each. *Courtesy of www.onthecornervintage.com.*

Beverage glass, Oregon, Hazel Atlas, 1950s, $6.00 – 8.00 each. *Courtesy of www. onthecornervintage.com.*

Beverage glass, map, Hazel Atlas, 1950s, $6.00 – 8.00 each. *Courtesy of www.onthecornervintage.com.*

Apron, floral with detachable bib, $10.00 – 15.00. *Courtesy of www. onthecornervintage.com.*

Primitive bowl, no markings, $15.00 – 20.00. Watermelon accessories new. *Courtesy of www.onthecornervintage.com.*

Cake carrier, plastic, Australia, 1950s, $15.00 – 18.00. *Courtesy of www.natashaburns.com.*

Tablecloth, fruit, no markings, good condition, $25.00. *Courtesy of www.onthecornervintage.com.*

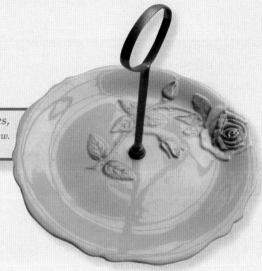

Cake plate, Royal Winton Grimades, Made in England, $80.00. Courtesy of www. natashaburns.com.

Vintage scale, Australian, $20.00. Courtesy of www.natashaburns.com.

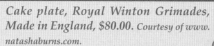

Kitchen cabinet, original paint, decals, $95.00 – 125.00. Courtesy of www.preservecottage.com.

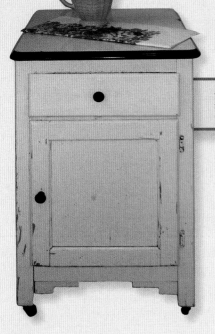

Kitchen cabinet, porcelain top, original paint, 1920s – 1930s, $40.00 – 75.00. *Courtesy of www.preservecottage.com.*

Hoosier cabinet, base only, 1930s, $275.00 – 375.00. *Courtesy of www.pinkpigwestport.com.*

On Deck

Antique ice cream bucket, original green paint, hand painted with roses by artist Jo-Anne Coletti of www.vintagerosec-ollection.com, $45.00, hand-painted with roses, $125.00.

Vintage metal thermometer, as found with old aqua paint, flea market find in Springfield, Ohio, 8" x 38", hand painted by artist Ronda Juniper Ray, $160.00.

Elmhurst Dairy aqua milk box, metal, $25.00 – 35.00. Courtesy of www.fadedrosecottage.com.

Hand-painted sign on reclaimed wood, $55.00 – 65.00. Courtesy of www.natashaburns.com.

Hand-painted vintage wood box, $65.00 – 75.00. Courtesy of www.natashaburns.com.

Plant stand, metal, $15.00 – 20.00.

Table, metal, hand painted, $75.00.
Courtesy of www.preservecottage.com.

Red, White & Blue

Pillow, striped, feather, marked,
"Made by L. Buchman Co., Inc.,
Brooklyn, N.Y.," 1955, $10.00 – 15.00.
Courtesy of www.onthecornervintage.com.

Planters, pretty blue pottery, $15.00 – 30.00 each. *Courtesy of Coffee Trade Antiques.*

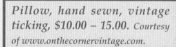

Pillow, hand sewn, vintage ticking, $10.00 – 15.00. *Courtesy of www.onthecornervintage.com.*

Pillows, pair, newly sewn from 1940s drapery damask, $20.00 – 25.00 each. *Courtesy of www.preservcottage.com.*

Birdfeeder, primitive, 1940s, $70.00 – 80.00. *Courtesy of www. pinkpigwestport.com.*

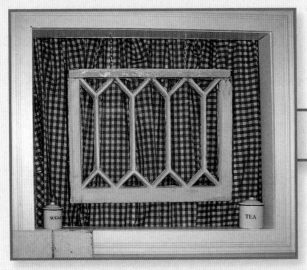

Vintage window sash as found $45.00 – 75.00. *Courtesy of www. ticklemepinkboutique.com.*

Rocker, country, painted, 1940s, $200.00 – 300.00. *Courtesy of www.pinkpigwestport.com.*

Sea captain statue, 1950s, $75.00. *Courtesy of www.pinkpigwestport.com.*

Window shelf, old window with added shelf, painted, $45.00. Courtesy of www.LisasCraftiqueBoutique.com.

Shelf made from old shutters, $25.00 – 45.00. Courtesy of www.LisasCraftiqueBoutique.com.

Shelf made from old shutters, painted, $25.00 – 45.00. Courtesy of www.LisasCraftiqueBoutique.com.

Shabby cabinet from vintage window and distressed wood, $45.00. Courtesy of www.LisasCraftiqueBoutique.com.

Sail Away

Tray, painted glass, 1950s, $45.00 – 50.00. Courtesy of www.pinkpigwestport.com.

Table made from old shutters, $45.00 – 65.00. Courtesy of www.LisasCraftiqueBoutique.com.

Salt and pepper shakers, google eyes, 1930s, $65.00 – 85.00 set. Courtesy of www.vintagepastelle.com.

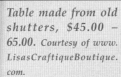

Salt & pepper shakers, no markings, sailboat motif, $50.00 – 60.00 set. Courtesy of www.onthecornervintage.com.

Wallpaper

All the samples of sailboat related novelty wallpaper are from www.hannahstreasures.com, a vintage wallpaper specialty company. When ordering from Hannah's Treasures, expect to pay about $95.00 – 110.00 a roll with prices rising as the demand for these products are increasing.

Seaside Views

Antique cast metal porthole window found at a flea market in Maine, artist Ronda Juniper Ray, $275.00.

Within this house
May God's love abide
To bless all those
who step inside

Antique window salvaged from an early twentieth century brick home in the historic German Village area of Columbus, Ohio, artist Ronda Juniper Ray, $350.00.

Leaded glass window from a 1935 brick four-square home in the historic district of Upper Arlington, Ohio, artist Ronda Juniper Ray, $225.00.

Ocean butterfly faux window oil painting, $375.00. *Courtesy of www.artfulcreations.biz.*

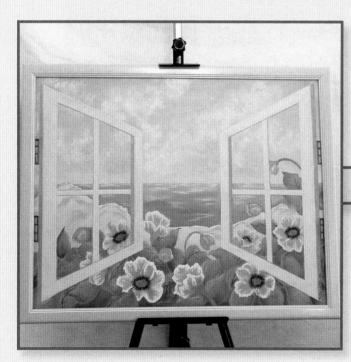

Ocean poppy faux window oil painting, $375.00. *Courtesy of www.artfulcreations.biz.*

Courtesy of www.pinkpigwestport.com.

Cabin Fever

Blankets & Blanket Pillows
Country Pillows
Decorative Accessories
Decorative Folk Art
Dressers: Dark Wood
Reclaimed Wood Furniture
Salvage: Windows
Signs
Trunks, Suitcases & Shelves
Wallpaper

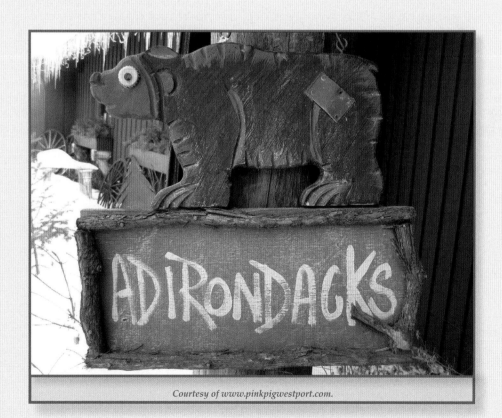

Courtesy of www.pinkpigwestport.com.

abin style living is hot, hot, hot! More and more people are talking about a desire to escape to the mountains, lake, or a favorite hideaway where cell phones lose their signal. One friend counts the days until he can retire and build a log cabin in the woods. A colleague dreams of his retreat cabin with a stone fireplace, wood planked floors, and a million dollar view of the hilltops. Books about tree houses, hideaways, camps, and cottages occupy more and more shelf space at the bookstores. Rustic is in and so are collectibles that are natural, original, chippy, rusted, weathered, rough, flaky, and primitive.

Requests for antique flooring of oak, chestnut, and pine, hand-hewn antique posts and beams as well as furniture made from reclaimed woods are rising. So is the call for vintage salvage items such as doors, windows, mantles, fireplaces, architectural trim, door knobs, bathtubs, stoves, and so much more.

Rustic retreats are back on the charts and so are the collectibles which go with this type of cottage or cabin style. When I am out hunting for collectibles I see other "junk-enthusiasts" with arms filled with old fishing baskets, snow shoes, bait pails, hunting gear, decoys, and vintage skis. The prices for decoys, folk art, Native American artifacts, Adirondack furniture, and collectible camp and sporting related accessories are climbing.

Collectors are also scooping up old trunks, boxes, signs, vintage suitcases, copper pots as well as and primitive kitchenwares and accessories. Beacon blankets and other textiles are in demand and often complement vintage beds, comfy sofas, and dark stained furnishings. Vintage wallpapers originally designed for boy's rooms in the 1940s and 1950s are used in cabins as decorative accents. I have included some beautiful examples of these wallpapers in the chapter entitled Holidays at the Cottage.

If you can't find enough rolls of wallpaper to cover the walls of an entire room, consider using vintage wallpaper to frame a fireplace or picture window. Or use novelty patterns to add interest to a collection of hunting gear, fishing rods, or lures. A vintage tartan plaid makes a great background for vintage golf clubs and sports memorabilia. Cozy, relaxed, and comfortable are what rustic retreats are all about.

Blankets & Blanket Pillows

Blankets, robes, and accessories made from old camp blankets are very collectible. Think again before you pass by the textiles in grandma's linen closet. Camp blankets were made with geometric, plain, and Indian designs. In the 1930s Indian blankets sold for $1.00 – 4.39 depending on whether they were cotton, wool, and had sateen trim. Today expect to pay $100.00 – 125.00 for early Indian or cowboy blankets in good condition. Blankets should be free of holes, without thin spots, and no "balling." Later blankets are made with nylon or synthetics and are valued less. Look for blankets made by the Beacon Manufacturing Co. of New Bedford, Massachusetts, and later of Swannanoa, North Carolina, or Pendleton Woolen Mills.

For more information on this topic be sure to read *Beacon Blankets* by Jerry & Kathy Brownstein. Vintage blankets are a wonderful edition to a cabin home. They are not only a practical collectible but add color and interest to a dark wood paneled room. You can also hang blankets on the wall, over the back of a sofa or chair, or keep your collection in a large basket or decorative wooden box on the floor. Cottage collectors love finding new ways to use vintage items. If you come across a damaged blanket consider making into a nice pillow or shawl.

Vintage Beacon blanket, 1930s, $125.00 – 200.00. Courtesy of www. pinkpigwestport.com.

Vintage Beacon blanket, 1930s, $125.00 – 200.00. Courtesy of www. pinkpigwestport.com.

Vintage Beacon blanket, 1930s, $125.00 – 250.00. Courtesy of www. pinkpigwestport.com.

Pillows, handmade from original Beacon blankets, $75.00 – 100.00 each. Courtesy of www.pinkpigwestport.com.

Country Pillows

The country pillows shown here are handmade by Barbara Smith of Buttons Buttons. Barbara takes pages from cloth children's books of the 1930s – 1950s and combines them with old feedsack cloths, ticking, and trim to create nostalgic decorative pillows popular in country cottages. Barbara also likes to create pillows by mixing vintage fabrics from camp and antique horse blankets, barkcloth, draperies, and embroidered French linens to complete a comfy cottage or cabin look. With a background in interior design, Barbara currently is busy at work in her textile studio located in a pre-Civil War house on the village green in Jay, New York. Pillows shown in this section are $75.00 – 85.00. Photographs courtesy of www.pinkpigwestport.com.

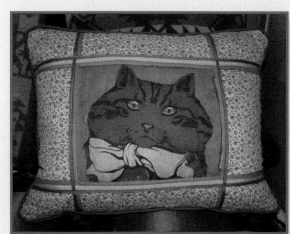

Porky The Pig

Decorative Accessories

Most of the decorative accessories in this section are from the collection of pinkpigwestport.com. Deb owns an antique shop in Westport, New York, as well as an online store. You can always contact her with your special request. She is terrific at finding customers country and rustic accessories and furnishings. Right now I have her scouting around for country store items for my group shop.

Bait pail, tin, 1940s, $65.00 – 75.00.
Courtesy of www.pinkpigwestport.com.

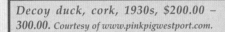

Decoy duck, cork, 1930s, $200.00 –
300.00. *Courtesy of www.pinkpigwestport.com.*

Pendant lamp, tin, 1930s, $150.00 –
200.00. *Courtesy of www.pinkpigwestport.com.*

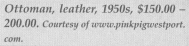

Ottoman, leather, 1950s, $150.00 – 200.00. *Courtesy of www.pinkpigwestport. com.*

Tub, rusted, probably used for coal or cinders, $25.00 – 45.00. *Courtesy of www. teacupsandtwigs.com.*

Old bottles, wicker covered, $20.00 each. *Courtesy of Coffee Trade Antiques.*

Frederic Remington print, 1940s, $50.00 – 75.00. Courtesy of www. pinkpigwestport.com.

Frederic Remington print, 1940s, $50.00 – 75.00. Courtesy of www. pinkpigwestport.com.

Adirondack backpack basket, 1940s, $150.00 – 250.00. Courtesy of www.pinkpigwestport.com.

Vintage Adirondack snow shoe, $75.00 – 85.00. Courtesy of www. pinkpigwestport.com.

Vintage cross country skis, 1940s, $200.00 – 250.00. Courtesy of www.pinkpigwestport.com.

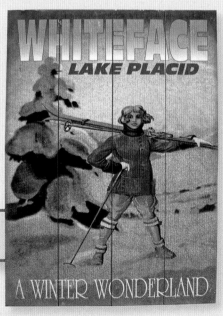

Sign, vintage Adirondack ski advertisement, $100.00 – 200.00. Courtesy of www.pinkpigwestport.com.

Asian wedding basket, $200.00 – 300.00.
Courtesy of www.pinkpigwestport.com.

Decorative Folk Art

Tin Ceiling Folk Art

Pressed or embossed tin ceilings were very popular during the Victorian era as an affordable substitute for the plaster designed ceilings found in wealthy European homes. Thin metal sheets of tin, copper, or stainless steel were stamped with intricate patterns and often painted white to resemble the more expensively produced hand carved or molded plaster ceilings. Companies in Ohio, New York, and Pennsylvania mass produced thin metal plate during the late 1800s and created numerous patterns to choose from.

Since tin ceilings are back in vogue again, there are many companies specializing in new tin ceilings with hundreds of patterns. How do you know if you are buying tiles or objects that are truly vintage. Older ceiling tin is heavier than the newer version with surfaces showing lots of rust, dents, chippy paint, rough scaly edges, and sharp nail holes. Although reproductions are made to look like the real thing, you will notice that the new items are lighter, smoother, and are simply too "perfect."

There are several groups of people interested in these tiles.

Some folks are after tiles for home restoration projects. Others are collectors who simply like collecting tiles in a variety of patterns and colors. A third group are artists and crafters who make handsome objets d'art out of these architectural finds.

The Pennsylvania Dutch are noted for creating barn stars out of old tin roof material.

Using reclaimed ceiling tin as decorative accessories in today's cottage homes is an excellent way to blend older traditions with modern day lifestyles.

The tin hearts shown are handmade from antique ceiling tins and crystal embellishments, re-created now, $50.00 – 60.00; iron bird hook, painted yellow, 1950s, $45.00 – 75.00. Courtesy of www.pinkpigwestport.com.

Wall hooks, mounted on antique ceiling tiles and painted, $30.00 – 35.00 each. Courtesy of www.pinkpigwestport.com.

Vintage sailor valentine box, shells and lithograph, 1800s, $250.00 – 500.00. *Courtesy of www.pinkpigwestport. com.*

Primitive weathervane, early 1900s, $700.00 – 1,000.00. *Courtesy of www.pinkpigwestport.com.*

Whirligig, primitive, whimsical, 1940s, $175.00 – 275.00; table, primitive, original paint, 1900s, $110.00 – 150.00. Courtesy of www.pinkpigwestport.com.

Planter, Adirondack, birch, 1940s, $65.00   95.00. Courtesy of www.pinkpigwestport.com.

Birdhouse, Adirondack, $45.00 – 65.00. Courtesy of www.pinkpigwestport.com.

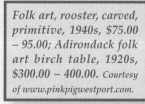

Folk art, rooster, carved, primitive, 1940s, $75.00 – 95.00; Adirondack folk art birch table, 1920s, $300.00 – 400.00. *Courtesy of www.pinkpigwestport.com.*

Polish hen, 1950s, $275.00 – 400.00; Adirondack folk art birch table, 1920s, $300.00 – 400.00. *Courtesy of www.pinkpigwestport.com.*

Folk art bird, 1950s, $200.00 – 300.00; table, primitive, original paint, 1800s, $150.00 – 250.00. *Courtesy of www.pinkpigwestport.com.*

Dressers: Dark Wood

In this section I have added photos of dressers in dark woods. You will also find more dressers in the chapter called

Sweet Shabby Dreams. Cabin owners like the darker look, but if you come across a dark dresser and prefer to see it repainted, if the price is right, go ahead and "shabby-tize it."

Period low boy dresser, late 1800s, $400.00 – 500.00. Courtesy of www.pinkpigwestport.com.

Victorian bonnet dresser, 1800s, $400.00 – 550.00. Courtesy of www.pinkpigwestport.com.

Federal dresser with original brass hardware, early 1900s, $400.00 – 500.00. Courtesy of www.pinkpigwestport.com.

Reclaimed Wood Furniture

All of the reclaimed wood furniture featured in this section is from the studio of Ed Goldberg, Connecticut. Ed Goldberg explained to me how so much interesting and wonderful wood is thrown out in the trash. Today collectors and crafters call this discarded wood "reclaimed." You can find reclaimed wood in a variety of settings. Wood from dismantled barns, farmhouses, remodeling jobs, etc. are increasingly sought after as homeowners are replicating older styles and seeking original woods for flooring, decorative trim, walls, etc. Buyers are able to obtain woods from businesses specializing in procuring and finishing older woods. Ed enjoys scouting for his finds directly, transforming old wood planks, quirky vintage cabinets, and found hardware into functional works of art. Ed looks at old wood like an artist looks at a blank canvas… deep in thought. Ed studies the wood for its natural textures, knots, burls, and unique characteristics. Then with a passion for handcrafted furniture, Ed creates one-of-a-kind furniture pieces which he says are timeless accents suitable for homes of all styles from rustic to contemporary to fresh vintage!

These one-of-a-kind pieces cross the category of "art" and "collectible" and are priced according to materials used, rarity, and complexity. For information about values email the author at Dianne@cdiannezweig.com.

Side table made of Appalachian ash, Rangeley log legs.

Side table, recycled nineteenth century chestnut with Rangeley log legs. Part of Arrow Collection. Resides in Maine summer camp.

Night table, handcrafted from nineteenth century chestnut flooring with Rangeley Maine log legs. Single drawer made from French wine crate.

Small table, 120-year-old Appalachian ash with original milk paint finish hand rubbed and waxed. This piece has an antiqued copper wave that gives good kharma. Handcrafted doweled joinery.

Small side table made of Rangeley birch legs, nineteenth century. Barn door featuring copper patina edge banding.

This rustic shelf piece can sit hutch style or hang on the wall. Made of 120-year-old Appalachian ash. Finish utilizes old milk paint with hand-rubbed stains. Detailed with antiqued copper strapping. $350.00.

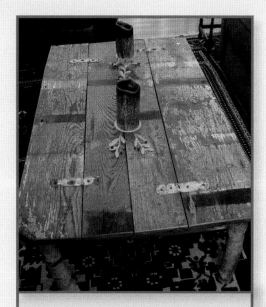

Coffee table, made of unusual nineteenth century distressed chestnut. Legs are of Rangeley Maine birch. Strap hinges are hand-wrought copper. The top opens for storage of magazines.

Bath shelf unit, features canoe arrow detail. Split hickory facing.

Cupboard bar chest, multi-use, handmade from nineteenth century barn door with hand-forged copper hinges and straps. Hand-carved arrow. Part of Arrow Collection. Multicolored hand-rubbed finish, $1,350.00.

Highboy chest of drawers, reclaimed wood. Doors and drawer facings are cut from new chestnut flooring. The case is white oak. Dawers open to shelves, and drawers are hand dovetailed. Hand-rubbed finish of Southwestern colors.

Farm table, three plank dining table made out of nineteenth century chestnut utilitizing original finish hand rubbed and waxed. Legs joined by splined and mahogany dowels finished with handmade chestnut nuts and handwrought copper daisy washers.

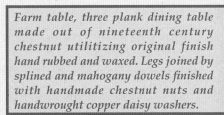

Outdoor porch camp table, made of ¾ quarter rough sawn slab edged pine. Part of hand-carved Arrow Series featuring Rangeley log legs.

Barn door coffee table with Rangeley white birch legs, hand-forged copper hinges and leg straps, $650.00.

Salvage Windows

Whether your preference is for the plain and simple farmhouse window, the elegant Victorian cathedral window, a soaring Palladian window, or a dramatic, pointed Gothic arch window, antique windows are stylish and charming and sure to be a focal point and conversation starter. Hung on the wall or leaning against a stone fireplace, antique windows are a singularly captivating element in any romantic room.

According to Rhonda Juniper Ray who is an artist who paints on antique windows, finding these windows is the fun part! She tells me that she is always on the prowl for unique and fabulous windows. She offers several suggestions to those of you hunting for salvaged windows. First, put out the word that you are looking for antique windows. Windows will come

knocking on your door, according to Rhonda. That is what happened when she moved into a small town with a lot of Victorian era homes in the area. She left her business card around town and was then contacted by a homeowner who was replacing the windows on his 1890s farm house. Rhonda offers another suggestion… knock on doors. If you see someone with replacement windows, ask them if they would like to sell the old ones. She says most of the time owners will gladly just give you the windows and be happy to have you take them off their hands. A third piece of advice is to establish relationships with folks at flea markets who are known dealers of salvage. Let them know what you are looking for so that the next time they clean out a house, they give you first dibs on the windows.

The salvaged window photographs in this section are the courtesy of Rhonda Juniper Ray, Port Austin, Michigan.

Arch-top window from a Great Smoky Mountains home in South Carolina, 32" x 39", $55.00.

Upper sash of a leaded glass double-hung window salvaged from a home in Lapeer, Michigan, 28" x 29", $65.00.

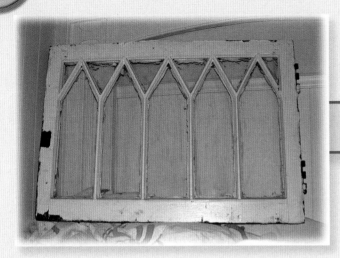

Window salvaged from an Arts and Crafts bungalow in Sunbury, Ohio. 36" x 25", $35.00.

One of a pair of windows salvaged from an Arts and Crafts bungalow in Marietta, Ohio, 27" x 41", $80.00 pair.

Window salvaged from a prairie foursquare in Millersport, Ohio, 40" x 29", $35.00.

Window salvaged from a farmhouse outside Chillicothe, Ohio, 33" x 39", $20.00.

Window salvaged from a barn outside Xenia, Ohio, 18" x 30", $20.00.

Window salvaged from a Colonial Revival home in Springfield, Ohio, 33" x 45", $300.00.

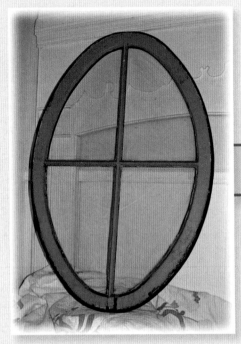

Window salvaged from a Colonial Revival home in York, Pennsylvania, 28" x 52", $150.00.

Window salvaged from a Gothic Revival home near Marysville, Ohio, 24" x 32", $50.00.

One of a pair of leaded glass windows salvaged from a Queen Ann Victorian in Delaware, Ohio, 40" x 24", $70.00 pair.

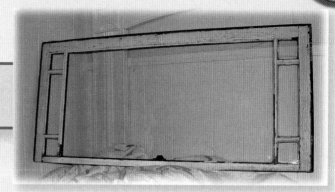

Window from a prairie foursquare in the historic Short North district of Columbus, Ohio, 53" x 24", $50.00.

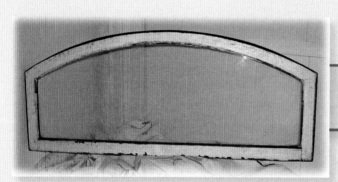

Transom salvaged from above the double front entry doors of an Italianate Victorian home in Springfield, Ohio, 54" x 22", $75.00.

Signs

Vintage signs priced right fly out of most antique shops. Porcelain enamel signs are "hot," especially "guy stuff" such as automobile and gas station themes. Signs come under the category of vintage advertising. You will find several different categories in this area, including porcelain enamel, flange signs, die-cut, self-framed, menu boards, counter displays, wood, tin, etc. Many tin signs have been reproduced so be cautious if the price seems too good to be true. On an older sign you would expect to see signs of age such as chipping, rust, worn surfaces, weathered surfaces, peeling paint, etc. Knowing where a sign came from is always helpful. Being lucky enough to acquire a local sign in a town that you are familiar with helps to weed out reproductions. Sometimes you come across a pretty good imitation of an older piece... if you love it, well of course buy it, just don't pay the same price you would for an original vintage sign.

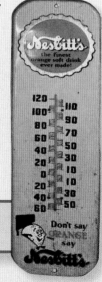

Advertising thermometer, Nesbitt's, 1930s, $225.00 – 325.00. *Courtesy of www.pinkpigwestport.com.*

Country sign, raised letters, 1950s, $200.00 – 300.00. *Courtesy of www.pinkpigwestport.com.*

Sign, Texaco, porcelain, 1937, $300.00 – 500.00. *Courtesy of www. pinkpigwestport.com.*

SNOWSHOE LODGE

Sign, Snowshoe Lodge, $100.00 – 200.00. Courtesy of www.pinkpigwestport.com.

Sign, Adirondack camp sign, $100.00 – 200.00. Courtesy of www.pinkpigwestport.com.

Trunks, Shelves & Suitcases

Suitcase, vintage, leather with travel stickers, 1940s, $75.00 – 80.00. Courtesy of www.pinkpigwestport.com.

Trunk, folk art, original paint, 1900s, $500.00 – 600.00. *Courtesy of www.pinkpigwestport.com.*

Captain's trunk, single plank oak, 1900s, $500.00 – 600.00. *Courtesy of www.pinkpigwestport.com.*

Trunk, folk art, original paint, 1900s, $500.00 – 600.00. *Courtesy of www.pinkpigwestport.com.*

Rustic chicken nesters, $85.00 – 120.00 each. Courtesy of www. teacupsandtwigs.com.

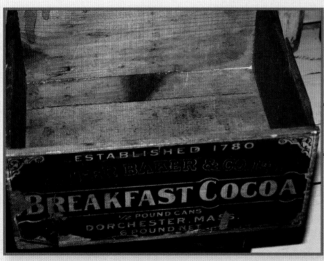

Old cocoa box with paper label, $25.00 – 45.00. Courtesy of www.teacupsandtwigs.com.

Wallpaper

All of the vintage wallpaper samples shown here are from the 1930s – 1950s and part of the portfolio of hannahstreasures. com. Hannah's Treasures, a vintage wallpaper company, carries a very large catalog of styles, eras, and textures. Owner Marilyn Krehbiel hand picked these lovely cottage and cabin prints to show readers the array of classic designs and patterns available. Warm tones and back to nature scenes are ideal wall coverings for retreat homes. Marilyn tells me that prices for rolls of wallpaper really vary a great deal, depending on whether you find full rolls or remnants at a flea market, online, in someone's attic, or from a specialty dealer. When ordering form Hannah's Treasures, expect to pay about $95.00 – 110.00 a roll with prices rising as the demand for these products are increasing.

Cabin Fever

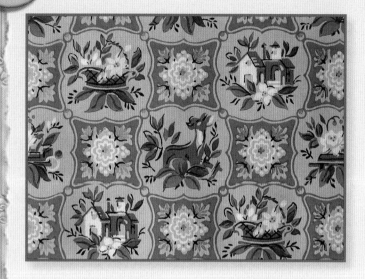

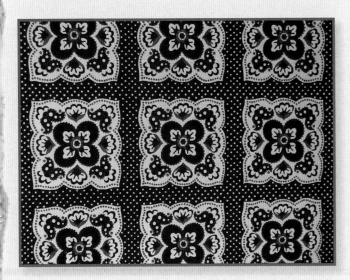

Courtesy of www.pinkpigwestport.com.

Holidays at the Cottage

Holiday Cottage Décor
Holiday Cottage Outdoor Décor
Holiday Figurines & Ornaments

Courtesy of www.pinkpigwestport.com.

Cottages look amazing during the holiday season. Somehow even the most contemporary homes take on a warm country vintage look during the holiday season. Ornaments, holiday serving pieces, décor, and textiles passed from one generation to the next are unpacked year after year and carefully placed throughout the home. Country collectibles mixed with natural materials such as leaves, twigs, tree branches, pine cones, berries, etc. are lovely easily obtainable ingredients for a fresh and cozy holiday. Vintage planters, tins, baskets, and vases can be used for floral arrangements, miniature trees, cookie and cake holders, etc. The key to cottage style is to be comfortable with what you own and to allow yourself free rein in experimenting with new ideas if you'd like.

Of course a real favorite hobby for so many at this time, is collecting older Christmas balls and ornaments to add to their established collections. At the Plantsville General Store Antiques Center in Plantsville, Connecticut, where I rent a booth to sell my antiques and collectibles, the small town and shops are transformed into a charming winter wonderland right after Thanksgiving.

Shortly after I sent my sisters back "to the city," following their annual pilgrimage "to the country" for Thanksgiving dinner this past year, I ventured into Plantsville. It was time to "decorate thy booth for the holidays." Since I celebrate Chanukah, it was a treat for me to borrow Christmas holiday ornaments from the co-op owner and carefully and strategically, I might add, decorate my booth. Like a young child looking through the elaborate holiday windows on Fifth Avenue in New York City, I was awed by the sparkle, color, and whimsy of our group shop at Christmas time.

Back home, I returned to my personal collection of menorahs, dreidels (spinning tops), holiday décor, and textiles. I too cherish the opportunity each year to unpack my favorite holiday items. I bring out the tablecloths that I serve my latkes (potato pancakes) on. I also delight in using a tin tray with a Chanukah design under my menorah to catch the candle drippings. I bought that round tin tray almost 25 years ago and never dreamed this inexpensive accessory would become a family treasure. The same is true for my favorite tablecloths.

These textiles have seen their share of spills, stains, and use, but I wouldn't even think of replacing them. Author Blu Greenberg cured me of worrying about stained tablecloths. I remember her pointing out that every time you add a new stain to a tablecloth think of it as representing all the precious times you spent with loved ones. If that doesn't calm you down the next time you spill some red wine… pour another glass!

The holidays are not only a time for collecting, but also for trying one's hand at homemade crafts. Vintage millinery supplies, buttons, lace, ribbons, wrapping paper, greeting cards, etc. are wonderful embellishments, supplies, and items which can be used as holiday décor or for gift wrapping. Janet, owner of The Country Cottage Florist & Antiques shop in Plantsville Connecticut, attaches a 1940s or 1950s Christmas card to the gift bags that shoppers carry out. What a sweet idea.

You will find many more lovely ideas in this section, from Adirondack style ornaments to holiday greetings painted on an old glass window. The photograph which opens this chapter shows candles sitting in salvaged spindles. Cottage style collectors are always very inventive, even during the holidays.

Holiday Cottage Décor

Vintage sled, painted, $45.00 – 65.00. *Courtesy of www.ticklemepinkboutique.com.*

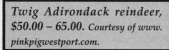

Twig Adirondack reindeer, $50.00 – 65.00. *Courtesy of www. pinkpigwestport.com.*

Antique spindles now candleholders, $15.00 – 25.00. *Courtesy of www.pinkpigwestport. com.*

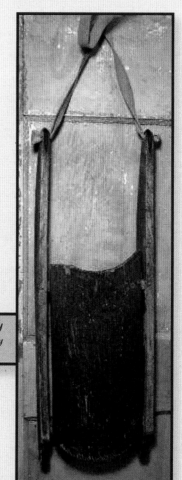

Sled, primitive, child's, early 1900s, $125.00 – 200.00. *Courtesy of www.pinkpigwestport.com.*

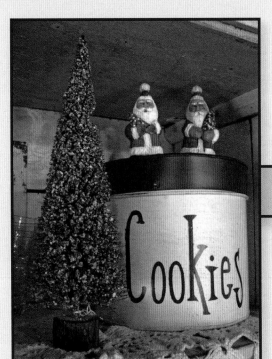

Bottle brush Christmas tree, 1950s, $15.00 – 25.00. Note: Cookie jar is not vintage. Courtesy of www.pinkpigwestport.com.

Vintage Santa sign, 1950s, $25.00 – 40.00. Courtesy of www. pinkpigwestport.com.

Vintage silk, stocking box with Christmas scene, 1930s, $30.00 – 45.00. Courtesy of www.pinkpigwestport. com.

Christmas hatbox set, 1950s, $75.00.
Courtesy of www.pinkpigwestport.com.

Salvaged window frame, 1900s,
$75.00 – 125.00. Courtesy of www.
pinkpigwestport.com.

Vintage advertising thermometer,
1950s, $35.00 – 45.00. Courtesy of
www.pinkpigwestport.com.

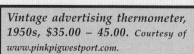

Vintage quilted Christmas
stocking, 1940s, $35.00 – 45.00.
Courtesy of www.pinkpigwestport.com.

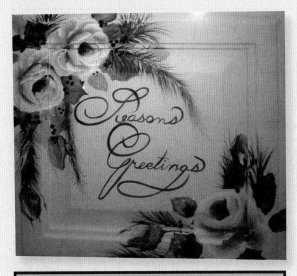

*Seasons Greetings painted on a vintage door
panel, pink cottage roses and Christmas greenery
adorn this piece, signed and dated by the artist,
1980s, $50.00. Courtesy of www.shabbycottagedesigns.com.*

*Leaded glass window from a 1935 brick
foursquare home in Upper Arlington,
Ohio, artist Ronda Juniper Ray, $275.00.*

Antique window salvaged from an 1880s farmhouse found at the end of a long, rutted, dirt road outside Lexington (Sanilac County), Michigan, artist Ronda Juniper Ray, $305.00.

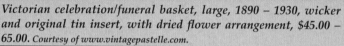

Victorian celebration/funeral basket, large, 1890 – 1930, wicker and original tin insert, with dried flower arrangement, $45.00 – 65.00. *Courtesy of www.vintagepastelle.com.*

Vintage basket, iron, original paint, 1940s, ornaments are a combination of Shiny Brites and German, 1940s, $8.00 – 20.00. *Courtesy of www.oldpainted-cottage.com.*

Tags, embellished with vintage buttons and jewelry pieces as well as new parts, $35.00 – 40.00 set of four. *Courtesy of www.soshabbypink.com.*

Old shoe form embellished with dried flowers, $15.00 – 25.00. *Courtesy of Coffee Trade Antiques.*

Holiday Cottage Outdoor Décor

Vintage Adironack wood moose, 1950s, $125.00 – 130.00.

Outdoor Christmas sled decoration, 1940s, large, wood, original paint, $125.00 – 175.00.

Outdoor ornament, snowman, 1950s, wood, original paint, $40.00.

Sled planter, 1920s – 1950s, wicker, metal, as found, $45.00. *Courtesy of www.vintagepastelle.com.*

Holiday Figurines & Ornaments

Vintage Christmas figurine planter, 1950s, $35.00 – 55.00. Courtesy of www. ticklemepinkboutique.com.

Vintage Christmas figurine, 1950s, $35.00 – 55.00. Courtesy of www.ticklemepinkboutique.com.

Vintage Christmas head vase, 1950s, $55.00 – 75.00. Courtesy of www.ticklemepinkboutique.com.

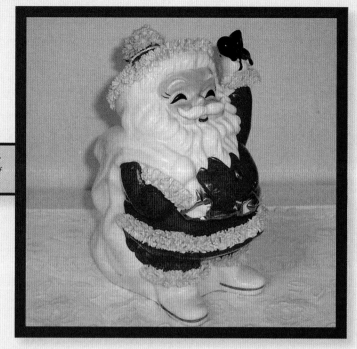

Vintage Christmas Santa bank, 1950s, $15.00   25.00. Courtesy of www.ticklemepinkboutique.com.

Frosted holiday tin star, $5.00 – 10.00. Courtesy of www. ticklemepinkboutique.com.

Vintage hand carved Santas, $35.00 each. Courtesy of www.pinkpigwestport.com.

Vintage Christmas Santa planter, 1950s, $15.00 – 25.00. Courtesy of www.ticklemepinkboutique.com.

Bibliography

Cottages

Allingham, Helen, and Stewart Dick. *The Cottage Homes of England*. New York: British Heritage Press, 1984.

Bass, Carol. *The Cottage Book: Living Simple and Easy*. New York: Stewart, Tabori & Chang, 2003.

Bix, Cynthia. *Cottage Style Decorating*. Menlo Park, CA: Sunset, 2003.

Caringer, Denise. *Better Homes and Gardens: Cottage Style*. Des Moines, IA: Meredith Publishing Group, 1998.

Clayton-Payne, Andrew. *Victorian Cottages*. London: Orion Publishing, 1997.

Coleman, Brian. *Classic Cottages: Simple, Romantic Homes*. Utah: Gibbs Smith, 2004.

English, Molly Hyde. *Vintage Cottages*. Utah: Gibbs Smith, 2007.

———. *Camps and Cottages*. Utah: Gibbs Smith, 2001.

Hilliard, Elizabeth. *Cottage English Country Style*. Boston: Bullfinch Press, 1994.

Plante, Ellen M. *Cottage Living: Designing Comfortable Country Retreats*. New York: Michael Friedman Publishing, 2000.

Schlang, Lisa Jill. *Cottage Retreats: Decorating Ideas for Every Mood*. New York: Michael Friedman Publishing, 2002.

Sheehan, Carol Sama. *Mary Emmerling's American Country Cottages*. New York: Clarkson Potter, 1993.

Zimmerman, Scott and Ann. *California Cottage Style*. New York: Sterling, 2005.

Cabins, Bungalows & Hideaways

Brown, Phil. *In the Catskills*. New York: Columbia University Press, 2002.

Carley, Rachel. *Cabin Fever: Rustic Style Comes Home*. New York: Simon & Schuster, 1998.

Faure, Sonya. *Hideaways: Cabins, Huts, and Tree House Escapes*. Paris: Flammarion, 2003.

LaBau, Peter. *The New Bungalow Kitchen*. Newtown, CT: Taunton Press, 2007.

Mulfinger, Dale, and Susan E. Davis. *The Cabin: Inspiration for Classic American Getaway*. Newtown, CT: Taunton Press, 2003.

Rosart, Sharyn. *Home Magazine: Best Little Houses*. New York: Michael Friedman Publishing, 1998.

Zillner, Dian, and Suzanne Silverthorn. *Cabin Style: Decorating with Rustic, Adirondack, and Western Collectibles*. PA: Schiffer Publishing, 2004.

Country Homes & Country Style

Atkins, Caroline. *Country Living: Shortcuts to Decorating Country Style*. New York: Hearst, 2004.

Innes, Jocasta. *Country Kitchens*. New York: Universe, 1996.

Plante, Ellen M. *Country Victorian*. New York: Michael Friedman, 1997.

Sheehan, Carol Sama. *Mary Emmerling's American Country Details*. New York: Clarkson Potter, 1994.

Wills, Margaret Sabo. *The Smart Approach to Country Decorating*. New Jersey: Creative Homeowner, 2001.

Shabby Chic, Flea Market, Vintage Style

Ashwell, Rachel. *Shabby Chic: Treasure Hunting & Decorating Guide*. New York: Harper Collins, 1998.

———. *Shabby Chic*. New York: Harper Collins, 1996.

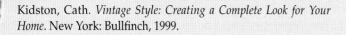

Kidston, Cath. *Vintage Style: Creating a Complete Look for Your Home*. New York: Bullfinch, 1999.

Strasser, Claudia. *The Paris Apartment*. New York: Harper Collins, 1997.

Tolley, Emelie, and Curtis Mead. *Flea Market Style: Decorating with a Creative Edge*. New York: Clarkson Potter, 1998.

Whitney, Sue, and Ki Nassauer. *Decorating Junk Market Style: Repurposed Junk to Suit Any Décor*. Des Moines, IA: Meredith, 2005.

General Decorating

Bartholomew, Kitty, and Kathy Price-Robinson. *Kitty Bartholomew's Decorating Style: A Hands-on Approach to Creating Affordable, Beautiful, and Comfortable Homes*. New York: Rodale, 2005.

Coleman, Brian D. *Details: How to Design with Architectural Salvage and Antiques*. Utah: Gibbs Smith, 2006.

DeMontravel, Jacqueline. *Romantic Homes: Vintage Vavoom*. New York: Clarkson Potter, 2007.

Freeman, John Crosby. *Victorian Style*. New York: Grange, 1991.

Hansgen, Karen. *The Nook Book: How to Create and Enjoy the Coziest Spot in the Home*. New York: Clarkson Potter, 2003.

Ho, Dan. *Rescue From Domestic Perfection*. New York: Bullfinch, 2006.

Huesten, Marie Proeller. *House Beautiful: Decorating With Books*. New York: Hearst, 2006.

Kennedy, Peggy. *Blue & White In Your Home*. New York: Hearst, 2001.

Moore, Kelly. *Cube Chic: Take Your Office Space from Drab to Fab*. Philadelphia: Quirk, 2006.

Poplar, Vitta. *Mary Engelbreit's Home Companion: Leading the Artful Life*. Kansas City, MO: Andrews McMeel, 2000.

Speert, Becky. *Great Color & Patterns Collections*. Des Moines, IA: Meredith, 2007.

Collections & Collectibles

Dahlstrom, Carol Field. *Collections: Projects & Ideas to Display Your Treasures*. Des Moines, IA: Meredith, 2002.

Garisto, Leslie. *Birdcage Book*. New York: Simon Schuster, 1992.

Louie, Elaine. *House Beautiful, Collections on Display: Decorating with Your Favorite Objects*. New York: Hearst, 2003.

Manroe, Candace Ord. *Designing with Collectibles: Creative Ideas for Collecting and Displaying Treasured Pieces in Your Home*. New York: Simon & Schuster, 1992.

Michels, Richard. *Collector's Style*. Des Moines, IA: Meredith, 2002.

Poplar, Vitta. *Mary Engelbreit's Home Companion: Collections*. Kansas City, MO: Andrews McMeel, 2000.

———. *Mary Engelbreit's Home Companion: Plates*. Kansas City, MO: Andrews McMeel, 1999.

Tuchman, Mitch. *Magnificent Obsessions: Twenty Remarkable Collectors in Pursuit of Their Dreams*. San Francisco, CA: Chronicle Books, 1994.

Whitesides, Mary. *Wicker Design*. Utah: Gibbs Smith, 2003.

Textiles

Atwood, Jennie Archer. *Sew Vintage: New Creations From Found Fabrics*. Newton, CT: Taunton, 2002.

Ganderton, Lucinda, and Rose Hammick. *Vintage Fabric Style*. New York: Ryland Peters & Small, 2003.

Poplar, Vitta. *Mary Engelbreit's Home Companion: Fabric*. Kansas City, MO: Andrews McMeel, 2001.

Psychology of Homes & Decorating

Marcus Cooper, Clare. *House: As Mirror of Self-Exploring the Deeper Meaning of Home*. Berwick ME: Nicolas-Hays, 1995.

Susanka, Sarah. *The Not So Big Life: Making Room For What Really Matters*. New York: Random House, 2007.

Contributors & Resources

Below is a list of the wonderful people who contributed photographs and information for this book or helped with the styling of photographs. I had a terrific time working with all of these successful and talented folks and hope you will visit their websites, shops, and antique malls.

A Rose Without a Thorn
www.arosewithoutathorn.com

Artful Creations
www.artfulcreations.biz

Bella Rosa Designs
www.bellarosadesigns.com

Bella Rose Cottage/Tres Chic Boutique
www.bellarosecottage.com

C'est Chouette Home
www.cestchouettehome.com

Carey Chelenza
www.dishnchips.com

Carol Morgan
Winsted, CT

Chris Lankford Collection
Ansonia, CT

Clinton Antique Center
Clinton, CT

Coffee Trade Antiques
Avon, CT
860-676-2661

Collinsville Antiques Co. of New Hartford
www.collinsvilleantiques.com

Cottage Rags
www.cottagerags.com

Country Cottage Chic
www.countrycottagechic.com

Country Cottage Florist
Plantsville, CT
860-621- 9858

Cynthia Cooper
www.antique-linens.com

Decorative Dishes
www.decorativedishes.net

Ed Goldberg's Furniture
Simsbury, CT

Elizabeth Holcombe
www.elizabethholcombe.typepad.com

Faded Rose Cottage
www.fadedrosecottage.com
www.paintedwhite.com

Fresh Vintage
www.freshvintagestyle.com

Greenville Cottage Antiques and Collectibles
www.indianvalley.net/greenville-cottage

Hannah's Treasures Vintage Wallpaper Collection
www.hannahstreasures.com

In The Pink Antiques
www.inthepinkantiques.com

Lavender Hill Studio
www.lavenderhillstudio.com

Lisa's Craftique Boutique
www.lisascraftiqueboutique.com

Nana Lulu's Linens and Handkerchiefs
www.nanaluluslinensandhandkerchiefs.com

Natasha Burns
www.natashaburns.com

On The Corner Vintage
www.onthecornervintage.com

Pink Pig Westport
www.pinkpigwestport.com

Plantsville General Store Antique Center
Elaine Maloney
www.pgsantiques.com

Preserve Cottage
www.preservecottage.com

Primrose Design
www.primrosedesign.com

Ronda Juniper Ray
www.antiquecottagerose.com

Retro-Redheads Vintage Linens & Housewares
www.retro-redheads.com

Romantic Rose Boutique
www.romanticroseboutique.com

Shabby Cottage Designs
www.shabbycottagedesigns.com

Shabbytown/Tickle Me Pink Boutique
www.ticklemepinkboutique.com

Shabby Villa
www.shabbyvilla.com

So Shabby Pink
www.soshabbypink.com

Stacy's Shabby Shoppe
www.stacysshabbyshoppe.com

Sweet Yesterdays
www.sweetyesterdays.com

Teacups & Twigs
www.teacupsandtwigs.com

The Bleu Willow
Simsbury, CT
860-264-1556

The Cottage Well Loved Furnishings
www.cottageatleesburg.com

The Old Painted Cottage
www.theoldpaintedcottage.com

The Vintage Nest
www.thevintagenest.com

Tickle Me Pink Boutique
www.ticklemepinkboutique.com
www.thedecalcottage.com

Urban Nostalgia
www.urbannostalgia.com

Vermont Salvage
www.vermontsalvage.com

Victoria's Vintage Shoppe
www.victoriasvintageshoppe.com

Vintage Pastelle
www.vintagepastelle.com

Vintage Pretty & Pink
www.vintageprettyandpink.com

Vintage Rose Collection
Jo-Anne Coletti
www.vintagerosecollection.com

more great TITLES from collector books

GLASSWARE & POTTERY

7362 American **Pattern Glass Table Sets**, Florence/Cornelius/Jones	$24.95
6326 **Collectible Cups & Saucers**, Book III, Harran	$24.95
6331 Collecting **Head Vases**, Barron	$24.95
7526 Collector's Encyclopedia of **Depression Glass**, 18th Ed., Florence	$19.95
6629 Collector's Encyclopedia of **Fiesta**, 10th Ed., Huxford	$24.95
5609 Collector's Encyclopedia of **Limoges Porcelain**, 3rd Ed., Gaston	$29.95
5842 Collector's Encyclopedia of **Roseville Pottery**, Vol. 2, Huxford/Nickel	$24.95
6646 Collector's Ency. of **Stangl Artware**, Lamps, and Birds, 2nd Ed., Runge	$29.95
7530 **Decorative Plates**, Harran	$29.95
7029 Elegant Glassware of the **Depression** Era, 12th Edition, Florence	$24.95
7638 Encyclopedia of **Universal Potteries**, Chorey	$29.95
7628 **English China** Patterns & Pieces, Gaston	$29.95
6126 **Fenton Art Glass**, 1907 – 1939, 2nd Edition, Whitmyer	$29.95
7630 **Fostoria Stemware**, The Crystal for America, 2nd Edition, Long/Seate	$29.95
6320 Gaston's **Blue Willow**, 3rd Edition	$19.95
6127 The **Glass Candlestick Book**, Vol. 1, Akro Agate to Fenton, Felt/Stoer	$24.95
7353 **Glass Hen on Nest Covered Dishes**, Smith	$29.95
6648 **Glass Toothpick Holders**, 2nd Edition, Bredehoft	$29.95
5840 **Heisey Glass**, 1896 – 1957, Bredehoft	$24.95
7534 **Lancaster Glass** Company, 1908 –1937, Zastowney	$29.95
7359 **L.E. Smith Glass** Company, Felt	$29.95
5913 **McCoy Pottery**, Volume III, Hanson/Nissen	$24.95
6335 Pictorial Guide to **Pottery & Porcelain Marks**, Lage, No values	$29.95
7637 **RumRill Pottery**, Fisher	$29.95
7623 Standard Encyclopedia of **Carnival Glass**, 11th Ed., Carwile	$29.95
6476 **Westmoreland Glass**, The Popular Years, 1940 – 1985, Kovar	$29.95

DOLLS & FIGURES

6315 **American Character Dolls**, Izen	$24.95
7346 **Barbie** Doll Around the World, 1964 –2007, Augustyniak	$29.95
6319 **Barbie Doll Fashion**, Volume III, 1975 – 1979, Eames	$29.95
6825 Celluloid Dolls, **Toys & Playthings**, Robinson	$29.95
7621 Collectible **African American Dolls**, Ellis	$29.95
6451 Collector's Ency. of **American Composition Dolls**, Vol. II, Mertz	$29.95
6546 Collector's Ency. of **Barbie Doll Exclusives**, 3rd Ed., Augustyniak	$29.95
6636 Collector's Ency. of **Madame Alexander Dolls**, 1948 – 1965, Crowsey	$24.95
6473 Collector's Ency. of **Vogue Dolls**, 2nd Ed., Izen/Stover	$29.95
6563 Collector's Guide to **Ideal Dolls**, 3rd Ed., Izen	$24.95
6456 Collector's Guide to **Dolls of the 1960s and 1970s**, Vol. II, Sabulis	$24.95
6944 Complete Gde. to **Shirley Temple Dolls** and Collectibles, Bervaldi-Camaratta	$29.95
7634 **Madame Alexander** Collector's Dolls Price Guide #33, Crowsey	$14.95
7536 Official **Precious Moments** Collector's Guide to Figurines, 3rd Ed., Bomm	$19.95
6467 **Paper Dolls** of the 1960s, 1970s, and 1980s, Nichols	$24.95
6642 20th Century **Paper Dolls**, Young	$19.95

JEWELRY & ACCESSORIES

4704 **Antique & Collectible Buttons**, Volume I, Wisniewski	$19.95
6122 Brilliant **Rhinestones**, Aikins	$24.95
4850 Collectible **Costume Jewelry**, Simonds	$24.95

5675 Collectible **Silver Jewelry**, Rezazadeh	$24.95
7529 Collecting **Costume Jewelry 101**, 2nd Edition, Carroll	$24.95
7025 Collecting **Costume Jewelry 202**, Carroll	$24.95
6468 Collector's Ency. of **Pendant & Pocket Watches**, 1500 – 1950, Bell	$24.95
6554 **Coro Jewelry**, A Collector's Guide, Brown	$29.95
4940 **Costume Jewelry**, A Practical Handbook & Value Guide, Rezazadeh	$24.95
5812 Fifty Years of Collectible **Fashion Jewelry**, 1925 – 1975, Baker	$24.95
6330 **Handkerchiefs**: A Collector's Guide, Guarnaccia/Guggenheim	$24.95
6833 **Handkerchiefs**: A Collector's Guide, Volume 2	$24.95
6464 Inside the **Jewelry Box**, Pitman	$24.95
7358 Inside the **Jewelry Box**, Volume 2, Pitman	$24.95
5695 **Ladies' Vintage Accessories**, Bruton	$24.95
7535 Mueller's Overview of American **Compacts & Vanity Cases**, No values	$29.95
1181 100 Years of **Collectible Jewelry**, 1850 – 1950, Baker	$9.95
6645 100 Years of **Purses**, Aikins	$24.95
6942 **Rhinestone Jewelry**: Figurals, Animals, and Whimsicals, Brown	$24.95
6038 **Sewing Tools** & Trinkets, Volume 2, Thompson	$24.95
6039 Signed Beauties of **Costume Jewelry**, Brown	$24.95
6341 Signed Beauties of **Costume Jewelry**, Volume II, Brown	$24.95
6555 20th Century **Costume Jewelry**, 1900 – 1980, Aikins	$24.95
4850 Unsigned Beauties of **Costume Jewelry**, Brown	$24.95

FURNITURE

6928 Early **American Furniture**: A Guide to Who, When, and Where, Obbard	$19.95
3906 Heywood-Wakefield **Modern Furniture**, Rouland	$18.95
7038 The Marketplace Guide to **Oak Furniture**, 2nd Edition, Blundell	$29.95

TOYS & MARBLES

2333 Antique & Collectible **Marbles**, 3rd Ed., Grist	$9.95
7523 **Breyer** Animal Collector's Guide, 5th Ed., Browell/Korber-Weimer/Kesicki	$24.95
7527 Collecting **Disneyana**, Longest	$29.95
7356 Collector's Guide to **Housekeeping Toys**, Wright	$16.95
7528 Collector's **Toy Yearbook**, Longest	$29.95
7355 **Hot Wheels**, The Ultimate Redline Guide Companion, Clark/Wicker	$29.95
7635 **Matchbox Toys**, 1947 to 2007, 5th Edition, Johnson	$24.95
7539 **Schroeder's** Collectible Toys, Antique to Modern Price Guide, 11th Ed	$19.95
6650 **Toy Car** Collector's Guide, 2nd Ed., Johnson	$24.95

PAPER COLLECTIBLES & BOOKS

6623 Collecting **American Paintings**, James	$29.95
7039 Collecting **Playing Cards**, Pickvet	$24.95
6826 Collecting Vintage **Children's Greeting Cards**, McPherson	$24.95
6553 Collector's Guide to **Cookbooks**, Daniels	$24.95
1441 Collector's Guide to **Post Cards**, Wood	$9.95
7622 Encyclopedia of Collectible **Children's Books**, Jones	$29.95
7636 The Golden Age of **Postcards**, Early 1900s, Penniston	$24.95
6936 **Leather Bound Books**, Boutiette	$24.95
7036 **Old Magazine Advertisements**, Clear	$24.95
6940 **Old Magazines**, 2nd Ed., Clear	$19.95
3973 **Sheet Music** Reference & Price Guide, 2nd Ed., Guiheen/Pafik	$19.95

1.800.626.5420 Mon. – Fri. 8 am – 4 pm CT   Fax: **1.270.898.8890**

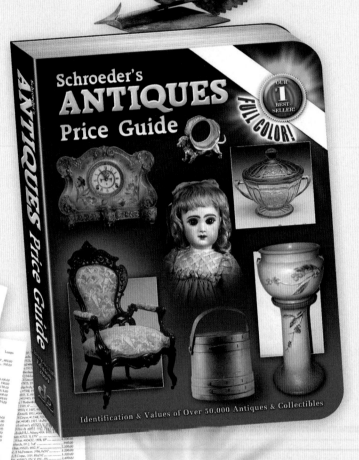